# STUDENT UNIT

## NEW EDITION

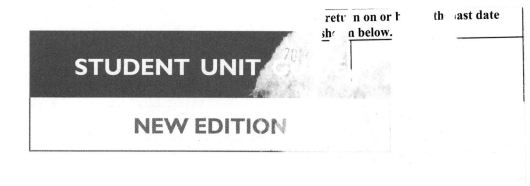

AQA(A) A2 Psych..log.. ...
(Sectio.. .)
Psychopat.. .o..

Jean-Marc ..w.on

Philip Allan Updates, an imprint of Hodder Education, an Hachette UK company, Market Place, Deddington, Oxfordshire OX15 0SE

*Orders*
Bookpoint Ltd, 130 Milton Park, Abingdon, Oxfordshire OX14 4SB
tel: 01235 827827
fax: 01235 400401
e-mail: education@bookpoint.co.uk
Lines are open 9.00 a.m.–5.00 p.m., Monday to Saturday, with a 24-hour message answering service. You can also order through the Philip Allan Updates website: www.philipallan.co.uk

© Jean-Marc Lawton 2012

ISBN 978-1-4441-6218-9
First printed 2012
Impression number 5 4 3 2 1
Year 2016 2015 2014 2013 2012

Cover photo: Ingram

Typeset by Integra, India

Printed in Dubai

Hachette UK's policy is to use papers that are natural, renewable and recyclable products and made from wood grown in sustainable forests. The logging and manufacturing processes are expected to conform to the environmental regulations of the country of origin.

P2037

# Contents

## Content Guidance

Specification content ● Clinical characteristics of schizophrenia ● Issues surrounding
the classification and diagnosis of schizophrenia ● Biological explanations of schizophrenia
● Psychological explanations of schizophrenia ● Biological therapies for schizophrenia
● Psychological therapies for schizophrenia

Specification content ● Clinical characteristics of depression ● Issues surrounding the classification
and diagnosis of depression ● Biological explanations of depression ● Psychological explanations of
depression ● Biological therapies for depression ● Psychological therapies for depression

Specification content ● Clinical characteristics of anxiety disorders ● Issues surrounding the
classification and diagnosis of anxiety disorders ● Biological explanations of anxiety disorders
● Psychological explanations of anxiety disorders ● Biological therapies for anxiety disorders
● Psychological therapies for anxiety disorders

## Questions & Answers

# Getting the most from this book

**Examiner tips**

Advice from the examiner on key points in the text to help you learn and recall unit content, avoid pitfalls, and polish your exam technique in order to boost your grade.

**Knowledge check**

Rapid-fire questions throughout the Content Guidance section to check your understanding.

**Knowledge check answers**

**1** Turn to the back of the book for the Knowledge check answers.

**Summary**

**Summaries**

- Each core topic is rounded off by a bullet-list summary for quick-check reference of what you need to know.

## Questions & Answers

**Exam-style questions**

**Examiner comments on the questions**
Tips on what you need to do to gain full marks, indicated by the icon ⓔ.

**Sample student answers**
Practise the questions, then look at the student answers that follow each set of questions.

**Examiner commentary on sample student answers**
Read the examiner comments (preceded by the icon ⓔ) following each student answer. Annotations that link back to points made in the student answers show exactly how and where marks are gained or lost.

AQA(A) A2 Psychology

# About this book

This guide will help you prepare for the AQA(A) A2 Psychology Unit 4 examination. It covers Section A of Unit 4, Psychopathology (Section B, Psychology in Action, and Section C, Psychological Research and Scientific Method, are covered in another book, 978-1-4441-7227-0), and is intended as a support device to revision and learning. The guide looks first at the specification content and how it is examined, and second at how answers of varying quality are assessed.

- The specification content for each topic is fully explained so that you understand what would be required from you in your examination (although other content may be equally appropriate).
- Content appropriate to each topic is outlined, to an extent that it would be possible to construct an answer to questions set on that topic.
- Sample questions for the topics are provided, along with an explanation of their requirements.
- Sample answers are also provided, along with examiner comments explaining the strengths and limitations of each answer.

## Using this guide

You can use this guide in a variety of ways.

- **During your course**, each time you start a new topic (e.g. biological explanations of schizophrenia), use the unit guide to give you a quick overview of what is involved; reread each topic at regular intervals as you are studying it in class.
- **When you start revising**, use the unit guide to review the specification areas you have studied (such as psychological therapies for depression). Use the unit guide to refresh your learning and consolidate your knowledge of each of the Unit 4 topics covered.
- **When practising for the examination**, use the Questions and Answers section. Ideally you should attempt the questions yourself before reading the sample answers and examiner's comments, and then compare your answer with the one given. If you do not have time for this, you should at least make brief plans that you could use as the basis of an answer to each question. Study the sample answer and the examiner's comments and then add the key points from them to your own answer or plan.

# Content Guidance

In this section, guidance is given on each of the three topics covered by this unit guide. Each subsection starts by providing an outline and explanation of what the specification demands. This is then followed by a more detailed examination of the theories, research studies and evaluative points that each subsection is made up of.

A general pattern for each topic is followed wherever appropriate, first providing an outline and explanation of what the specification demands. The subject matter is then described, research evidence given and, finally, further evaluative points made. It is important to remember that research evidence can be used either as descriptive material when answering examination questions (AO1) or as evaluation (AO2/AO3). It is advisable to learn how to make use of such material in an evaluative way — for instance, by using such wording as 'this supports' and 'this suggests'.

For the research quoted here, names of researchers and publication dates are given. Full references for these should be available in textbooks and via the internet if you desire to study them further.

# Schizophrenia

## Specification content

- *Clinical characteristics of the chosen disorder*
- *Issues surrounding the classification and diagnosis of the disorder, including reliability and validity*
- *Biological explanations of the disorder, for example genetics, biochemistry*
- *Psychological explanations of the disorder, for example behavioural, cognitive, psychodynamic and sociocultural*
- *Biological therapies for the disorder, including their evaluation in terms of appropriateness and effectiveness*
- *Psychological therapies for the disorder, for example behavioural, psychodynamic and cognitive behavioural, including their evaluation in terms of appropriateness and effectiveness*

There will be one optional question on schizophrenia on the examination paper. To ensure that you can answer it, you need to study and understand all of the above.

Clinical characteristics refer to symptoms and types of schizophrenia that a sufferer may experience and you need a good working knowledge of these. Symptoms are listed within classification systems and you should also have a knowledge and understanding of issues of reliability (consistency) and validity (accuracy) associated with classifying and diagnosing schizophrenia.

Biological and psychological explanations are listed on the specification, so you need to cover both, though the specific explanations given (e.g. psychodynamic) are listed

**schizophrenia** a mental disorder characterised by withdrawal from reality

only as examples, meaning that they would not feature explicitly in any examination question. This also means that any other explanations, as long as they are biological or psychological, would be equally acceptable to study.

Finally, the specification focuses on biological and psychological therapies. Again the specific therapies referred to are listed only as examples, meaning that they cannot feature directly in any examination question and that any other therapies, as long as they are biological or psychological, would be equally acceptable to study. There is also a requirement here to be able to evaluate both biological and psychological therapies in terms of how appropriate and effective they are.

# Clinical characteristics of schizophrenia

The term schizophrenia literally means 'split-mind' and it is popularly seen as a condition where someone has two distinct selves or personalities, like a 'Jekyll and Hyde' character. However, this is a common misconception and is a description that better fits multiple personality disorders.

The term schizophrenia was first coined by Bleuler (1911) to mean 'divided self', and replaced Kraepelin's (1898) earlier term of dementia praecox. Schizophrenia is best described as a condition where personality loses its unity — like a jigsaw where all the pieces are there, but have been put together in the wrong order.

Schizophrenia seems to have existed for a long time, with historical references in many cultures to apparently schizophrenic behaviour. People from all sections of society and all cultures seem to be at risk of developing schizophrenia, though with differences in incidence rates. Overall just less than 1% of people worldwide suffer from schizophrenia, but prevalence rates vary between 0.33% and 15%. Any valid explanation of the disorder must be able to explain these facts.

Schizophrenia is the world's most common mental disorder, accounting for 40–50% of all mental patients. It is difficult to compile accurate statistics concerning the disorder, due to inadequately agreed criteria for diagnosis. Indeed estimates of how many schizophrenics there are in the world vary from 24 to 55 million people.

A good working definition of schizophrenia is that of Stafford-Clarke (1964): 'Schizophrenia is a generic name for a group of disorders, characterised by a progressive disintegration of emotional stability, judgement, contact with and appreciation of reality, which produces considerable secondary impairment of personality, relationships and intellectual functioning.'

Schizophrenia therefore is a serious mental disorder that affects a person's thought processes and ability to determine reality. The degree of severity varies among sufferers: some experience only one episode; some have persistent episodes, but are enabled to live relatively normal lives by taking medication; others have persistent episodes that do not respond to medication and therefore remain severely disturbed. It may be the case that schizophrenia is actually a group of disorders, with different causes and explanations. Indeed clinicians tend to distinguish Type I schizophrenia and Type II schizophrenia. Type I is an acute type characterised by positive symptoms, such as thought disorders. Type II schizophrenia is a chronic type characterised by negative symptoms, such as apathy, and has a poorer prospect of recovery.

**Type I schizophrenia**
acute form of schizophrenia characterised by positive symptoms and responsiveness to medication

**Type II schizophrenia**
chronic form of schizophrenia characterised by negative symptoms and unresponsiveness to medication

For a person to be diagnosed as schizophrenic, two or more symptoms must be apparent for more than one month, as well as reduced social functioning. Symptoms can be positive, where an excess or distortion of normal functioning occurs, or negative, where there is a lessening or loss of normal functioning. It is also possible to differentiate between chronic onset schizophrenia, where a person gradually withdraws and loses motivation over a prolonged period, eventually becoming more disturbed, and acute onset schizophrenia, where symptoms appear suddenly, usually after a stressful incident.

The onset of schizophrenia most commonly occurs between 15 and 45 years of age; there is an equal incidence rate between males and females, though males tend to show onset at an earlier age than females.

## Symptoms

Schneider (1959) detailed the First Rank Symptoms of schizophrenia, to which Slater and Roth (1969) made several additions.

- **Passivity experiences and thought disorders:** thoughts and actions are perceived as under external control (e.g. by other humans, by aliens). Sufferers may also believe thoughts are being inserted, withdrawn or broadcast to others.
- **Auditory hallucinations:** sufferers experience voices inside their heads, which can form a running commentary, or may appear to discuss the sufferer's behaviour.
- **Primary delusions:** sufferers usually first experience **delusions of grandeur**, feeling they are someone important (e.g. Jesus Christ reincarnated). Later, delusions may become **delusions of persecution**, where sufferers believe someone is out to get them. Some sufferers may experience only one type of delusion.
- **Thought process disorders:** sufferers wander off the point, or their words may become muddled, or new words and phrases can be invented.
- **Disturbances of affect:** sufferers may appear indifferent to others, or exhibit inappropriate emotional responses, or display huge mood changes.
- **Psychomotor disturbances:** sufferers may adopt frozen, statue-like poses, or exhibit tics and twitches, or repetitive behaviours.
- **Lack of volition:** sufferers display an inability to make decisions, have no enthusiasm and may not display any affection.

## Subtypes of schizophrenia

There is no such thing as a 'normal' schizophrenic exhibiting the 'usual' symptoms and so several subtypes of the disorder have been proposed. The ICD-10 classification system lists seven subtypes, while the DSM-IV classification system has five.

**(1) Paranoid:** this subtype is characterised by delusions of grandeur and/or persecution and there is less noticeable disturbance than with other subtypes. This is the one subtype many practitioners agree is a separate subtype.

**(2) Catatonic:** sufferers can be excitable and occasionally aggressive, but at other times they may be mute and adopt statue-like poses; they can even alternate between these two states. Negativism may be apparent, where sufferers do the opposite of what they are told. Hallucinations and delusions are less obvious.

**(3) Disorganised (hebephrenic):** onset normally occurs in the early to mid twenties, with sufferers experiencing auditory hallucinations, delusions, thought process disorders and disturbances of affect. Behaviour can appear bizarre.

**Knowledge check I**

Explain the difference between Type I and Type II schizophrenia.

**Examiner tip**

For questions asking for an outline of clinical characteristics of schizophrenia, use could be made not only of descriptions of clinical characteristics but also of symptoms and subtypes, as these also can be considered to contain elements of clinical characteristics.

**(4) Residual:** sufferers will have exhibited symptoms previously, but are not doing so at present, though negative symptoms will have been experienced during the past year. Generally sufferers display mild positive symptoms.

**(5) Undifferentiated:** this is basically a category for schizophrenics who do not fit any other subtype, or have symptoms of several subtypes.

**(6) Simple (found only in ICD-10):** this often appears in late adolescence with a slow, gradual onset. There is an increase in apathy and social deterioration occurs, along with a decline in academic or occupational performance.

**(7) Post-schizophrenic depression (found only in ICD-10):** this is a subtype for schizophrenics meeting criteria for the disorder in the last year, though not at present, who exhibit severe and prolonged depressive symptoms.

# Issues surrounding the classification and diagnosis of schizophrenia

This section deals with issues of reliability and validity in relation to the classification and diagnosis of schizophrenia.

## Reliability

Reliability refers to the consistency of measurements and affects the classification and diagnosis of schizophrenia in two ways:

- **Test–retest reliability** occurs when a practitioner makes the same consistent diagnosis on separate occasions from the same information.
- **Inter-rater reliability** occurs when several practitioners make identical, independent diagnoses of the same patient.

Even with physical medical disorders, diagnoses are not always reliable, and making reliable diagnoses of schizophrenia is more problematic, as the practitioner has no physical signs but only symptoms (what the patient reports) to base a decision on.

**Knowledge check 2**
Explain why there is no such thing as a 'normal' schizophrenic exhibiting the 'usual' symptoms.

**reliability** the consistency of diagnosis

### Research

- Beck et al. (1962) reported a 54% concordance rate between experienced practitioners' diagnoses when assessing 153 patients, while Söderberg et al. (2005) reported a concordance rate of 81% using DSM-IV-TR, the most up-to-date form of the DSM classification system. This suggests classification systems have become more reliable over time. As Nilsson et al. (2000) found only a 60% concordance rate between practitioners using the ICD classification system, it also suggests that the DSM system is more reliable.
- Read et al. (2004) reported test–retest reliability of schizophrenia diagnosis to have only a 37% concordance rate; they also noted a 1970 study where 194 British and 134 American psychiatrists were asked to provide a diagnosis on the basis of a case description: 69% of the Americans diagnosed the disorder as schizophrenia, but only 2% of the British did. This suggests that the diagnosis of schizophrenia has never been reliable.
- Seto (2004) reported that the term schizophrenia had been replaced by 'integration disorder' in Japan due to the difficulty of attaining reliable diagnosis, suggesting that schizophrenia, as a separate, identifiable disorder, does not exist.

- Jakobsen et al. (2005) tested the reliability of the ICD-10 classification system in diagnosing schizophrenia. A hundred Danish patients with a history of psychosis were assessed using operational criteria, and a concordance rate of 98% was attained, demonstrating the high reliability of the clinical diagnosis of schizophrenia using up-to-date classifications.
- Rosenhan (1973) got healthy participants to present themselves at psychiatric hospitals and report hearing voices, and generally they were diagnosed as schizophrenic and admitted. The only people who doubted their insanity were fellow patients. Practitioners quite reasonably protested they were not in the habit of trying to identify fakes and deny people access to hospital, so Rosenhan warned them that a number of pseudo-patients would try to gain admittance during a specified 3-month period. Out of 193 patients admitted, 41 were identified as fakes and a further 42 were suspected of being fakes. All were genuine patients, suggesting the reliability of schizophrenia diagnosis to be poor.

**Knowledge check 3**

What has research suggested about the reliability of diagnosis of schizophrenia?

## Evaluation

- The DSM classification system (used in the UK) is often regarded as more reliable than ICD, because of the degree of specificity in the symptoms outlined for each category.
- The reliability of schizophrenia diagnosis (+0.81) is superior to that for anxiety disorders (+0.63).
- Even if reliability of diagnosis based on classification systems is poor, they do at least allow practitioners to have a common language, permitting communication of research ideas and findings, which may ultimately lead to a better understanding of the disorder, and effective treatments.
- Evidence generally suggests that the reliability of diagnoses has improved as classification systems have been updated.

## Validity

**validity** the accuracy of diagnosis

Validity concerns how accurate, meaningful and useful diagnosis is. There are a number of ways in which validity can be assessed, for instance:

- **Reliability:** a valid diagnosis has first to be reliable (though reliability itself is no guarantee of validity).
- **Predictive validity:** if diagnosis leads to successful treatment, then the diagnosis can be seen as valid.
- **Descriptive validity:** for diagnosis to be valid, patients diagnosed with different disorders should actually differ from each other. Descriptive validity is reduced by comorbidity, where patients are seen as having two or more disorders simultaneously, suggesting that such disorders are not actually separate from each other.
- **Aetiological validity:** for diagnosis to be valid, all patients diagnosed as schizophrenic should have the same cause for their disorder.

## Research

- Heather (1976) argues that very few causes of mental disorders are known and there is only a 50% chance of predicting what treatment a patient will receive based on diagnosis, suggesting diagnosis of schizophrenia has low validity.
- Allardyce et al. (2006) report that the symptoms used to characterise schizophrenia do not define a specific syndrome — rather, a number of different combinations and permutations of the defining symptoms are possible, suggesting that schizophrenia is not a separate disorder and that therefore diagnosis of the disorder is invalid.
- Dikeos et al. (2006) used factor analysis to correlate symptoms, and found diagnostic entities are similar with regard to the key symptom dimensions, thus suggesting diagnosis of the disorder does have validity.
- Hollis (2000) studied 93 cases of early onset schizophrenia, applying DSM classification diagnoses retrospectively to patient case notes. The findings indicated that the diagnosis of schizophrenia had a high level of stability, suggesting such diagnoses are to a large extent valid.
- Bottas (2009) reports that the incidence of schizophrenia in the population is about 1% and that of obsessive–compulsive disorder (OCD) is about 3%. However, the incidence of schizophrenia with OCD is much higher than probability would suggest. Genetic and neurobiological evidence now indicates that there may be a separate schizo-obsessive disorder, which in turn suggests that separate types of schizophrenia may indeed exist.
- Jansson and Parnas (2007) reviewed 92 polydiagnostic studies, which apply different definitions of the disorder to the same patient samples, to assess the reliability and validity of schizophrenia diagnoses. Both ICD-10 and DSM-IV showed moderate reliability, but both were weak on all measures of validity, again casting doubt on whether the disorder exists as a separate condition.

## Evaluation

- Bentall (2003) says the diagnosis of schizophrenia tells us nothing about the cause of the disorder, implying diagnosis to be therefore invalid. Also diagnosis tells us nothing about prevalence rates, which differ widely from rural to urban environments, again suggesting diagnosis to be invalid.
- Kraepelin (1898) saw schizophrenia as a chronic deteriorating condition in all cases. This is not true, with many outcomes possible, from complete recovery to chronic suffering, again suggesting diagnosis to be invalid.
- The diagnosis of schizophrenia bestows a stigma upon a sufferer that has a huge and long-lasting negative impact on his or her life. Once applied, the label is hard to get rid of and yet such diagnosis may be made with very little evidence of validity in terms of the condition actually existing as a separate one.
- Kendell and Jablensky (2007), in response to the argument that schizophrenia should be abolished as a concept because it is scientifically meaningless, state that diagnostic categories are justifiable concepts, as they provide a useful framework for organising and explaining the complexity of clinical experience, allowing us to derive inferences about outcome and to guide decisions about treatment.
- Whaley (2004) believes that cultural bias is the main reason that the incidence of schizophrenia is greater among black Americans than white Americans, as ethnic

**Knowledge check 4**

What has research indicated about the validity of diagnosis of schizophrenia?

**Examiner tip**

Students often confuse the relationship between reliability and validity. A valid diagnosis must be reliable (consistent), but a reliable diagnosis does not guarantee validity (accuracy). For example, adding up 1 + 1 several times and always getting the answer 3 is reliable but not valid. Adding up 1 + 1 several times and always getting 2 is, however, both reliable and valid.

differences in symptom expression are overlooked or misinterpreted by practitioners. This suggests a lack of validity in diagnosing schizophrenia cross-culturally.

- Cochrane (1977) reported that the incidence of schizophrenia in the West Indies and Great Britain is the same, at around 1%, but that people of Afro-Caribbean origin are seven times more likely to be diagnosed as schizophrenic when living in Great Britain. This suggests either that Afro-Caribbean people living in Great Britain experience more stressors leading to schizophrenia, or that invalid diagnoses are being made due to cultural bias.

# Biological explanations of schizophrenia

biological explanations
perceiving a condition as
having a physiological cause

Biological explanations have focused on several areas, including genetics, evolution, biochemistry, neuroanatomy and pregnancy factors. Although the causes of schizophrenia are still not fully understood and indications are that several contributory factors may combine to cause the onset of the disorder, the evidence does suggest that biological factors play a major contributory role.

## Genetic explanations

genetic explanation
perceiving a condition
to be transmitted by
hereditary means

Research has traditionally used twin, family and adoption studies to assess what role, if any, a genetic explanation might play in the causation of schizophrenia. Results from all sources indicate schizophrenia to have a genetic component, although one of the problems with such studies is separating out environmental influences.

More recently, technology has advanced, allowing gene mapping studies to be undertaken. This entails comparing genetic material from families with a high incidence of schizophrenia and families with a low incidence of the disorder. Results from gene mapping indicate that several genes rather than just one gene are probably involved and that what genes do is make some individuals more vulnerable than others to developing the disorder. Therefore genes probably do not cause schizophrenia on their own: indeed, if they did, the concordance rate between MZ (monozygotic, or identical) twins would be 100%, which it clearly is not.

### Research

- Torrey et al. (1994) reviewed evidence from twin studies, finding that if one MZ twin develops the condition, there is a 28% chance the other twin will too.
- Gottesman and Shields (1976), reviewing five twin studies, reported a concordance rate of between 75% and 91% for MZ twins with severe forms of schizophrenia, suggesting genetics may play a larger role with chronic forms of the disorder.
- Kety and Ingraham (1992) identified schizophrenics who had been adopted and compared the prevalence of the disorder in their genetic and adoptive relatives, finding schizophrenia to be ten times higher among genetic relatives. This suggests that genetic factors play a much greater role than environmental factors. However, this research has been criticised (see evaluation below).
- Sorri et al. (2004) performed a longitudinal study over 21 years on Finnish adoptees who had biological mothers with schizophrenia, comparing them with adoptees without schizophrenic mothers. However, family rearing styles among adoptive families was also considered. It was found that adoptees at

high genetic risk of developing the disorder are significantly more sensitive to non-healthy rearing patterns, suggesting that environmental factors as well as genetic ones are important.

- Varma and Sharma (1993) found a concordance rate of 35% for first-degree relatives of schizophrenics, compared to only 9% in first-degree relatives of non-schizophrenics, indicating a major contributory role for genetic factors.
- Parmas et al. (1993) conducted a longitudinal family study of schizophrenia, finding 16% of children with schizophrenic mothers went on to develop the disorder, compared to only 2% of children without schizophrenic mothers, suggesting schizophrenia to be more genetic than environmental.
- Gurling et al. (2006) used evidence from family studies indicating schizophrenia was associated with chromosome 8p21-22, to identify a sample with a high risk of developing the condition. Using gene mapping, it was found that the PCM1 gene was implicated in susceptibility to schizophrenia, suggesting another source of evidence for the genetic argument.
- Benzel et al. (2007), using gene mapping, have found evidence that NRG3 gene variants may interact with both NRG1 and ERBB4 gene variants to create a susceptibility to developing schizophrenia, suggesting an interaction of genetic factors.

**Examiner tip**
When revising material for the psychopathology section of your Unit 4 examination, ensure that you have prepared material for both a short and a longer version of answers requiring an outline. Sometimes an outline may be worth just 4 marks, but at other times 8 marks. A different amount of material would therefore be required for these questions.

## Evaluation

- Twin studies suggest a genetic factor in the onset of schizophrenia, but such studies often do not consider the influence of social class and socio-psychological factors.
- Twin studies also tend to produce conflicting evidence, with heritability estimates ranging from 58% for MZ twins, suggesting a large contributory role for genetics, to as low as 11%, suggesting a much lesser role.
- Leo (2006) argues that Kety and Ingraham's adoption study evidence is not as convincing as first appears. First, sample sizes were very small, making generalisation difficult; and second, many of the biological relatives found to have schizophrenia were quite distant relatives (e.g. half-siblings), with low biological similarity.
- Hedgecoe (2001) believes scientists have attempted to construct schizophrenia as a genetic disease by using evidence from twin and adoption studies in a biased way to 'produce a "narrative" about schizophrenia which subtly prioritizes genetic explanations'.
- Varma and Sharma (1993) believe family studies can be used to identify samples for further research that have an increased probability of carrying the schizophrenic genotype.
- Although family studies tend to support the genetic viewpoint, they often fail to consider shared environmental influences, lessening support for a genetic explanation.
- Overall, the findings from studies involving genetics provide strong evidence for the **diathesis–stress model**, where individuals inherit different levels of genetic predisposition to developing schizophrenia, but ultimately it is environmental triggers that determine whether an individual actually goes on to develop the disorder.

- Gene mapping offers the possibility of developing tests to identify people with a high risk of developing schizophrenia, though this could raise a wide range of socially sensitive and ethical concerns.
- Tosato et al. (2005) conducted a review of gene mapping and similar studies, concluding that it is highly likely there are several genes involved in susceptibility to schizophrenia. This suggests schizophrenia does not have a singular genetic cause.

## Evolutionary explanations

Schizophrenia continues to be apparent in the population and there is historical evidence that it has existed for a very long time. These facts suggest that it may have an adaptive value and therefore an evolutionary explanation. If the disorder served no useful purpose, then the evolutionary viewpoint would argue that the process of natural selection would have selected it out and it would no longer exist. This view of the origins of schizophrenia is therefore very different in that the condition is perceived not as maladaptive but as fulfilling a beneficial purpose.

Stevens and Price (1997) have proposed the **group splitting hypothesis**, according to which schizophrenia is an occasionally necessary attribute to ensure the success of newly formed human groups and therefore continues to be represented in the gene pool. Humans are seen as thriving and multiplying within an environment until the group reaches a critical size where there are not enough resources to sustain it successfully. At this point the group splits and successful, dynamic leadership of the new factional groups is essential if they are to survive and prosper. Such leaders need to possess schizophrenic-like qualities, such as communication with 'higher' or 'god-like' beings, charisma, high energy and delusions of grandeur.

### Research

- Burns (2002) reviewed evidence from several fields and proposed that schizophrenia is a disorder of cortical and specifically fronto-temporal connectivity, which evolved under selective pressures involving group living. Schizophrenia exists therefore as a costly trade-off in the evolution of social cognition and the creative mind.
- Peters et al. (1999) studied British religious cults, finding leaders to be charismatic and to possess high levels of near-psychotic delusional beliefs, suggesting that in the ancestral environment schizophrenic traits may have played a significant role in the splitting and dispersal of people.
- Storr (1997) cites a number of modern examples of group leaders possessing schizotypal, paranoid, psychopathic qualities, such as David Koresh, Jim Jones and Adolf Hitler.
- Polimeni and Reiss (2002) propose that schizophrenia evolved because characteristics associated with it, such as communicating with spirits or possessing supernatural powers, enhanced the ability of a shaman (spiritual group leader) to perform spiritual ceremonies. This suggests that schizophrenia served as a behavioural specialisation during human evolution.

**evolutionary explanation** perceiving a condition as having an adaptive purpose linked to survival

**Examiner tip**

When describing biological explanations of schizophrenia, such as the evolutionary explanation, it may be necessary to outline the explanation in general, for example that evolutionary explanations see an adaptive advantage to human qualities and behaviours. However, answers that are not specifically oriented at explaining how evolutionary theory views schizophrenia will earn little, if any, credit.

## Evaluation

- Larson and Nyman (1973) found schizophrenics to have lower fertility rates, while Brown (1997) found them to have increased earlier mortality. Therefore the disorder seems maladaptive and by the laws of natural selection should have disappeared from the gene pool long ago. The fact that it has not implies some adaptive advantage.
- The theory is difficult to test as evidence tends to be retrospective and lacking in empirical support.
- Although a fair number of leaders can be said to possess schizophrenic-like qualities, it is clear that the majority of leaders do not, even in new, breakaway social groupings, somewhat weakening support for the theory.

# Biochemical explanations

The biochemical explanation of schizophrenia centres on the idea that the neurotransmitter **dopamine** is connected to the onset of the disorder. Neurotransmitters are chemicals found within the body which are associated with the transmission of signals through the nervous system, especially the sending of signals across the gaps between nerve fibres during the process known as synapse. The dopamine theory of Snyder (1976) proposes that, during the synaptic process, too much dopamine is released, leading to the onset of the disorder, with sufferers showing extremely high numbers of D-2 receptors on receiving neurons, which causes increased dopamine binding and makes more neurons fire.

The theory was developed after it was discovered that phenothiazines, antipsychotic drugs that lessen the symptoms of schizophrenia, inhibit dopamine activity. Additionally, the dopamine-releasing drug L-dopa tends to create schizophrenic-like behaviour in people who are not psychotic. Other drugs that influence the dopaminergic system, such as the powerful hallucinogenic LSD, also create schizophrenic-like behaviour in non-psychotics and aggravate symptoms in those susceptible to the disorder. It is also possible that genetic factors may be involved in creating faulty dopaminergic systems in schizophrenics.

Davis et al. (1991) updated the original theory, which was seen as too simplistic because high levels of dopamine were not found in all schizophrenics and because the modern anti-schizophrenic drug clozapine, which has very little dopamine-blocking activity, works very effectively against the disorder. Therefore it was now suggested that high levels of dopamine in the mesolimbic dopamine system are associated with positive symptoms, while high levels in the mesocortical dopamine system are associated with negative symptoms.

Interest has also more recently focused on the neurotransmitter **glutamate**, as there is reduced function of the NMDA glutamate receptor in schizophrenics. It may be abnormal glutamate functioning that is more associated with the onset of the disorder, with dopamine involved too, as dopamine receptors inhibit the release of glutamate.

**biochemical explanation** perceiving a condition as being determined by the actions of neurotransmitters and hormones

**Examiner tip**
An excellent way of producing high-quality answers to questions on explanations of schizophrenia is to illustrate how factors can be combined. For example, with biochemical explanations, the neurotransmitter glutamate can be offered as a sole explanation but can also be combined with dopamine to offer a more sophisticated explanation as to how they collectively influence the experience of schizophrenia.

**Research**

- Iversen (1979) reported that post-mortems on schizophrenics had found an excess of dopamine in the limbic system, suggesting the neurotransmitter to be involved in the disorder.
- Randrup and Munkvad (1966) induced schizophrenic-like behaviour in rats by giving them amphetamines, which activate dopamine production, and then reversed the effects by giving them neuroleptic drugs, which inhibit the release of dopamine.
- Kessler et al. (2003) used PET and MRI scans to compare schizophrenics with non-sufferers and found schizophrenics had significantly elevated dopamine receptor levels in the basal forebrain and substantia nigra/ventral tegmental brain areas. Differences in cortical dopamine levels were also found, suggesting that dopamine is an important factor in the onset of schizophrenia.
- Javitt et al. (2000) found that glycine, a glutamate receptor agonist, reversed phencyclidine hydrochloride induced psychosis (which closely resembles schizophrenia) in rats and made schizophrenics better, lending support to the glutamate theory.

## Evaluation

- Differences in the biochemistry of schizophrenics could be an effect rather than a cause of the condition.
- Healy (2000) believes pharmaceutical companies were keen to see the dopamine theory promoted, as they would make huge profits from manufacturing anti-schizophrenic drugs that inhibited dopamine production.
- The theory cannot explain why sufferers given neuroleptic drugs recover only slowly, when the medication has an instant effect on dopamine levels.
- Lloyd et al. (1984) believe that, even if dopamine is a causative factor, it may act indirectly, because abnormal family circumstances may lead to high levels of dopamine that in turn trigger the symptoms.

**Knowledge check 5**

How do the following biological explanations perceive the causes of schizophrenia: (a) the genetic explanation; (b) the evolutionary explanation; (c) the biochemical explanation?

**neuroanatomical explanation**
perceiving a condition as being determined by abnormalities in brain structures

## Neuroanatomical explanations

Enlargement of the ventricles (cavities that hold cerebrospinal fluid) has been found in the brains of some schizophrenics after death, suggesting a possible neuroanatomical explanation. As this seemed to be true only of schizophrenics who did not respond to drug treatment, there was a belief that such enlarged ventricles were an effect of being severely disturbed over many years, leading to physical brain damage. The introduction of MRI scans made it possible to study live brains and structural abnormalities have indeed been located in many schizophrenics, especially those with Type II (chronic) schizophrenia, indicating that there may be more than one type of the disorder — though again there is the possibility that structural abnormalities develop over time in those who experience a worsening of symptoms. What has been difficult to establish is whether structural abnormalities precede the onset of the disorder, indicating schizophrenia to be a developmental condition, or whether they occur gradually as a result of the disorder.

**Research**

- Torrey (2002) reported the discovery of enlarged ventricles in schizophrenic brains, which may be the result of reduced development in certain brain areas.
- Kim et al. (2000), using MRI scans, found that some schizophrenics have small frontal lobes and abnormal blood flow in certain brain areas, again suggesting that reduced development in the brain may be associated with schizophrenia.
- Green (2001) found that structural differences most commonly occur in the frontal lobes, the hippocampus and the temporal lobes, with these differences being linked to the cognitive deficits that commonly occur in schizophrenics, such as problems with memory, attention and problem solving.
- Spencer et al. (2004) reported poor gamma-band activity in EEG recordings from schizophrenics, suggesting weak integration of neural networks in the brain, with those who had the most severe delusions and hallucinations showing the lowest activity.

## Evaluation

- Dean (1999) reported that it may be the use of neuroleptics to treat schizophrenia that leads to structural abnormalities and that therefore the structural abnormalities have little if anything to do with the onset of schizophrenia.
- Brown (2006) believes neuroanatomical abnormalities may occur because of early neurodevelopmental changes arising due to factors associated with pregnancy.
- Findings from MRI scans suggest schizophrenia is associated with structural abnormalities, but different studies cannot agree as to which brain areas are affected.
- As MRI scans tend to be done on sufferers after they have developed the condition, it is not known whether structural damage occurs before or after the onset of schizophrenia.

# Pregnancy factors

A curious fact about schizophrenia is that many sufferers are born in the winter months. This means that sufferers in the northern and southern hemispheres tend to be born at different times of the year, because winter occurs at different times in the two parts of the world. As viral infections often occur during wintertime, interest has centred on whether such infections contracted during pregnancy may make unborn children more vulnerable to developing the disorder in later life. Perhaps structural and biochemical abnormalities associated with the onset of schizophrenia can be traced not to a genetic basis, but to damage during pregnancy or from birth complications.

**pregnancy factors** perceiving a condition as being determined by infections and complications to fetuses during pregnancy

**Research**

- Khashan et al. (2008) used the Danish register of births to identify 1.38 million births between 1973 and 1995, and found that children born to mothers who experienced severe stress in early pregnancy (such as the death of a loved one) had a 67% increased risk of developing schizophrenia, suggesting pregnancy factors may be involved in the onset of the disorder.

- Geddes (1999), reviewing research concerning pregnancy and schizophrenia, concluded that there is evidence linking pregnancy complications, such as underweight fetuses and bleeding during pregnancy, with the later development of schizophrenia in males. It was suggested that reduced placental function impairs fetal brain development, leading to heightened vulnerability.
- Murray (1996) put forward the flu theory, which was based on his observation that the children of women who contracted flu during pregnancy incurred an 88% increased chance of developing schizophrenia compared to children born in the same period to mothers who did not contract flu. Murray also believes people of Afro-Caribbean descent living in Britain are five times more likely to develop schizophrenia than in their country of origin, because they have little immunity to flu, while people of Asian descent living in Britain do not experience heightened rates of schizophrenia, as they do have immunity to the virus.
- Torrey et al. (1988) reported that surges in rates of schizophrenia correspond closely to flu pandemics, supporting the idea that such viruses are involved in the development of the disorder.

## Evaluation

- Not everyone whose mother experienced birth or early pregnancy complications goes on to develop schizophrenia, implying that other factors must also be involved.
- Much of the evidence linking pregnancy and birth complications to schizophrenia is correlational, so causality cannot be established.
- Although evidence has linked flu to schizophrenia, the risk is small, with 97% of babies born to women who had flu while pregnant not developing the disorder.
- Ploeger (2008) believes that schizophrenia and autism share the common origin of disorders in early pregnancy, with both disorders often leading to similar physical abnormalities, like peculiar toes. In early development, organogenesis occurs with a lot of interaction between different bodily parts. Therefore if something goes wrong with one part of the body, then other parts are affected too, suggesting the foundation for psychiatric disorders is laid in early pregnancy.

**Knowledge check 6**

How do the following biological explanations perceive the causes of schizophrenia:
(a) neuroanatomical explanations;
(b) pregnancy factors?

**psychological explanations** perceiving a condition as having non-physiological causes

**behaviourist explanations** the determination of a condition through learning processes

# Psychological explanations of schizophrenia

Although evidence indicates that biological factors play an important role in the onset of schizophrenia, it is generally accepted that psychological factors are also involved. There are several psychological explanations of schizophrenia, including the behaviourist, psychodynamic, cognitive and sociocultural explanations.

## Behaviourist explanations

Behaviourist explanations see schizophrenia as a learned condition and therefore do not perceive the disorder as a mental illness with a physical cause. Operant conditioning may be involved, with people being reinforced (rewarded) for abnormal behaviour and thus learning bizarre behaviours. Additionally, bizarre behaviour may be rewarding due to the attention it brings, with an increase in such behaviour eventually leading to psychosis. Alternatively, retreating to an inner world may be rewarding as an escape from real-world pressures, leading to such people being labelled as schizophrenic and then behaving so as to meet the requirements of the label.

Behaviourism explains the tendency of schizophrenia to run in families in social learning terms, as being merely a result of observing and imitating affected family members.

**Research**

- Scheff (1966) reported that people behaving bizarrely come to be aware of their label of schizophrenic and play the role of a mentally ill person, perhaps inadvertently at first but, later, voluntarily. Therefore a group of actually short-lasting symptoms comes to be stabilised, through self-consciousness and reaffirmation by others, as a 'career' of mental illness.
- Ullman and Krasner (1969) reported that staff in hospitals reinforced schizophrenic behaviour in their patients, paying more attention to those who displayed characteristics of the disorder. The patients saw that, if they disobeyed and played up, the staff would make a fuss over them.
- Tarrier et al. (1988) found that schizophrenics randomly assigned to behavioural intervention treatments had lower relapse rates than those receiving more usual treatments, suggesting a behavioural component to the onset of the disorder.
- Liberman (1982) reported that children may learn to be schizophrenic by being reinforced for bizarre responses to inappropriate stimuli and such reinforcements lead to even more bizarre behaviour and, eventually, psychoticism.

## Evaluation

- Token economy, a treatment used with schizophrenics whereby they are rewarded with tokens (exchangeable for desired goods) for exhibiting more 'normal' behaviour, has met with general success, implying some support for behaviourist explanations.
- The symptoms and associated behaviours of schizophrenia may be too bizarre and distressing to be imitative and brought on merely by labelling, though for a few such labelled schizophrenics this may be true.
- Meehl (1980) dismissed the behaviourist explanation, noting the behaviour of a patient who 'kept his finger up his arse to stop his thoughts escaping, simultaneously tearing his hair out, as it was his father's', and questioning how such behaviour could be brought about simply by being labelled schizophrenic.
- Behaviourism cannot explain why many schizophrenics exhibit similar symptoms without ever having witnessed such behaviour before, or why the disorder tends to first occur in late adolescence or early adulthood.

## Psychodynamic explanation

The psychodynamic explanation believes schizophrenics have regressed to a state of primary narcissism, whereby they have no ego to allow them to experience reality. The cause is seen as being an increase of sexual urges during early adulthood, or

**Examiner tip**
With 24-mark questions requiring an outline and an evaluation (e.g. 'Outline and evaluate explanations of schizophrenia'), students can spend too long on the outline, leaving little time for evaluation. The outline is worth only 8 marks while the evaluation is worth 16 marks, so spend one-third of the time on the outline and two-thirds on the evaluation.

**psychodynamic explanation** perceiving a condition as determined by regression to an infantile state of earlier childhood development maybe an increase in aggressive urges (the neo-Freudian view). The explanation proposes that schizophrenics have experienced either interpersonal regression or interpersonal withdrawal, and stress is seen as a major contributory factor, with an emphasis also on the personality characteristics of parents, the interactions between parents and children, and family structures.

Fromm-Reichmann (1948) has theorised the possible existence of **schizophrenogenic** mothers, women who are cold and controlling and who create a rearing environment characterised by tension and secrecy that leads to children developing the disorder.

### Research

- Klein and Bion (1946) proposed that all children go through an early stage that is characterised by feelings of omnipotence and persecution, and if a child has a poor relationship with their primary caregiver then they will not progress from this stage and will possess a schizophrenic core of personality. Such individuals, as adults, respond to stress by regressing to their earlier state of persecution and omnipotence, classic symptoms of schizophrenia.
- Read et al. (2005) reviewed studies of schizophrenia and found a link between sexual abuse in childhood and later development of schizophrenia and also that schizophrenia was the most common mental disorder for victims of sexual abuse, lending some support to the psychodynamic explanation.
- Hammersley et al. (2003) found that the hallucinations experienced in schizophrenia were especially linked to abuse in childhood, suggesting further support for the explanation.
- Koopmans (1997), reviewing studies of the disorder, found greater interactional ambiguity in families that include a schizophrenic member, especially between sufferers and their mothers, than in families without a schizophrenic member, again lending support to a psychodynamic explanation.

## Evaluation

- There is little in the way of empirical data to back up the psychodynamic theory and most evidence comes from subjective analyses of case studies, which also rely upon honesty and accuracy of recall during psychoanalysis.
- Gottesman (1991) stated that although evidence pointed towards a genetic factor underlying schizophrenia, the contribution of the rearing environment could not be ignored in the search for the origins of schizophrenia.
- Most sufferers of schizophrenia have not suffered abuse as children, sexual or otherwise, so this cannot be seen as explaining all cases of schizophrenia.

### Knowledge check 7

How do the following psychological explanations perceive the causes of schizophrenia:
(a) behaviourist explanations;
(b) psychodynamic explanations?

**cognitive explanation**
schizophrenia perceived as determined through maladaptive thought processes

## Cognitive explanations

The cognitive explanation sees maladaptive (faulty) thinking as strongly linked to schizophrenia, and many of its symptoms, such as hallucinations and disordered thinking, suggest a cognitive input. This could occur directly or indirectly: for example, brain abnormalities may lead to the experience of hallucinations.

A particular focus of interest has been the role of attention, with the possibility that schizophrenics cannot filter out irrelevant sensory information and so are bombarded with data that they cannot interpret meaningfully, therefore experiencing a sensory world different from that of others.

Hemsley (1993) proposed that a breakdown occurs between information already stored in memory and new incoming data. Stored information is used to create schemas that allow us to interpret and deal with current situations but in schizophrenics, due to the breakdown in cognitive processing, such schemas are not activated, sensory overload occurs and the sufferer cannot determine what to attend to and what to ignore. This leads to delusional thinking and, because thoughts do not seem to originate from memory, they can often be interpreted as arising externally.

Frith (1992) similarly wanted to explain schizophrenia in terms of problems with information processing and was especially interested in **metarepresentation**, the ability to reflect on thoughts and experience, and **central control**, the ability to suspend automatic responses and instead perform actions based on conscious intent. The positive symptoms of schizophrenia, such as delusions, are seen as problems of metarepresentation where there is an inability to distinguish external speech from internal thoughts. Conversely, negative symptoms, such as disorganised thinking, are seen as problems of central control, where there is a failure to distinguish between behaviour of conscious intent and that of automatic response.

### Research

- Frith (1970) gave schizophrenic and non-schizophrenic participants a two-choice task where they had to guess whether the next playing card in a pack was red (R) or black (B). Schizophrenics produced stereotypical choices, like RRRRRR or RBRBRB, while non-schizophrenics produced more random choices, suggesting schizophrenics have problems generating spontaneous actions, thus supporting the idea of negative symptoms resulting from a lack of central control.
- Liddle and Morris (1991) found that schizophrenics perform poorly on the Stroop test, where the desire to name the colour in which a word is written has to be suppressed in order to read out the actual word. This suggests that the positive symptoms of schizophrenia involve a failure of willed action, with behaviour therefore being determined by irrelevant stimuli.
- Robinson and Becker (1986) propose that neuronal circuits involving the limbic system participate in schizophrenics' inability to integrate moment-to-moment sensory inputs with stored memories as per Hemsley's theory (see above). Distress is seen as leading to increased dopamine production, which in turn influences the functioning of these brain areas, suggesting a link between biological and cognitive factors.
- Bentall et al. (1991) found schizophrenics struggled to identify words from a certain category (e.g. birds) as ones which they had read earlier, ones they had created themselves or ones they had not seen before, supporting Frith's theory that schizophrenics have metarepresentation problems.

### Examiner tip

A useful way to evaluate both explanations and therapies is to compare different ones, drawing out their appropriateness and effectiveness by contrasting their relative strengths and weaknesses. Questions may even ask for such a comparison, such as 'Critically compare biological and psychological explanations of schizophrenia.'

## Evaluation

- Garety et al. (2001) believe that schizophrenia will be best understood by linking together different explanations, both biological and psychological, and that cognitive explanations are a vital link in this chain.
- Hemsley (1996) argues that cognitive models allow schizophrenia to be linked to its neural bases and that this creates opportunities for useful therapies to be constructed.
- Kane and Lencz (2008) propose that the inclusion of cognitive impairment in the diagnostic criteria for schizophrenia would greatly increase the validity of diagnosis and would improve treatment by targeting cognitive enhancement as a primary goal.
- Camozzato and Chaves (2002) report that cognitive impairments are not found in a uniform fashion among schizophrenics, supporting the possibility of the existence of different subtypes of the disorder.

## Sociocultural explanations

sociocultural explanations
schizophrenia perceived as determined through family and social environments

Sociocultural explanations are based upon social and cultural factors, such as the family and social environments. Other psychological explanations can also be seen in sociocultural terms — for example, labelling theory sees the label of schizophrenia as a social phenomenon.

The degree of expressed emotion within a family (hostility, over-concern, etc.) is seen as a strong indicator of relapse in schizophrenics and thus as a social factor contributing to the maintenance of the disorder.

Another proposed sociocultural explanation is the double-bind theory, where schizophrenia is seen as a learned response to conflicting messages and mutually exclusive demands during childhood. Over time this leads to disorganised thinking and communication.

Another aspect is social causation: the lower social classes, who are subject to more stressors, have higher levels of schizophrenia, suggesting that this may be a causal factor.

### Research

- Leff (1976) reported a relapse rate of 51% for schizophrenics returning to homes with high expressed emotion compared to only 13% for schizophrenics returning to homes with low rates of expressed emotion.
- Haley (1981) found unclear, confusing and conflicting communication patterns in families of schizophrenics, suggesting it was these expressed emotions that contributed to the development and persistence of the disorder.
- Hjern et al. (2004), using data from a national cohort study in Sweden, found that social adversity in childhood was associated with an increased risk of developing schizophrenia, lending support to the social causation viewpoint.
- Cooper (2005) found that the Afro-Caribbean population in Britain experience many social difficulties in their lives, such as urban living, unemployment and separation from family, suggesting it is these social factors that explain the heightened vulnerability to schizophrenia in this population.

## Evaluation

- An alternative explanation to the social causation viewpoint is that of downward drift, where schizophrenia results in reduced social status and thus the sufferer drifts down through society into the lower classes.
- Sociocultural factors may be effects rather than causes of schizophrenia: for instance, expressed emotions may occur within a family due to the stresses and conflicts involved in living with a schizophrenic rather than contributing to the condition's onset.
- If high expressed emotion within families is deemed to be a contributory factor in developing schizophrenia, then this suggests treatments should be targeted at changing this element within families, rather than targeting schizophrenics themselves.
- Haller (1989) concluded, after reviewing evidence from research into the double-bind theory, that it was extremely difficult to evaluate its worth as an explanation due to methodological constraints.

# Biological therapies for schizophrenia

This section discusses ECT and drug treatment as biological therapies used for schizophrenia.

## ECT

Electro-convulsive therapy (ECT) was first introduced as a treatment for schizophrenia by Cerletti (1935) on the false basis that inducing an epileptic fit would remove the symptoms of schizophrenia, as the two conditions cannot exist together. Over time this was deemed not to be an effective treatment but, more recently, ECT has been reintroduced as a treatment for schizophrenia and is currently regarded as more effective than placebos, though not as effective as drug therapies. ECT seems to work best when applied bilaterally (to both sides of the head). Treatments are given in conjunction with an anaesthetic and a muscle relaxant.

**Research**
- Tharyan and Adams (2005) reviewed 26 studies of ECT treatment for schizophrenia, concluding that it is a fairly effective treatment in the short term, being better than no treatment but not as good as antipsychotic drugs.
- Tharyan (2006) reviewed studies of ECT treatments and concluded there was some evidence for the short-term relief of schizophrenic symptoms, but the treatment was best when used in conjunction with drug treatments.
- Tang et al. (2002) found ECT to be effective in treating schizophrenics who did not respond positively to treatment with antipsychotic drugs, suggesting the treatment can provide some relief to such patients.
- Fisk (1997), reviewing clinical literature, concluded that ECT has a success rate of 60–80% but is only effective against certain categories of schizophrenia, and more treatments (between 20 and 30) are needed than with other disorders.

**Knowledge check 8**
How do the following psychological explanations perceive the causes of schizophrenia: (a) cognitive explanations; (b) sociocultural explanations?

**biological therapies** treatments of schizophrenia that are based upon physical methods of intervention

**electro-convulsive therapy (ECT)** a treatment for schizophrenia that involves the application of electrical voltages across the brain

**Knowledge check 9**
What does research suggest about the effectiveness of ECT as a treatment for schizophrenia?

**Examiner tip**

When evaluating therapies it is creditworthy to comment on ethical considerations. For example, are schizophrenics, in their mentally disordered state, truly able to give informed consent to receive ECT? An elaboration of this point could refer to a cost–benefit analysis, for instance the lack of informed consent considered against the fact that treatment may bring relief from the disorder.

**drug therapy** the chemical treatment of schizophrenia through tablets and intravenous means

**Examiner tip**

Research that finds therapies effective can be used to positively evaluate such therapies but can, additionally, be used to support the explanations on which they are based. Therefore, research detailing the success of drug therapies also backs up the biological approach. However, the treatment aetiology fallacy states that the fact that drugs alleviate symptoms does not necessarily mean they are treating the cause.

## Evaluation

- Between 20% and 50% of schizophrenics who respond positively to ECT relapse within 6 months, suggesting that it does not offer a long-term solution to treating the disorder.
- Unilateral ECT treatment produces fewer side effects, such as short-term memory loss, but is not as effective as bilateral treatment in treating the disorder. Memory generally returns to normal, but 1% suffer severe memory loss.
- ECT has a bad image to shake off, as its usage can seem brutal and be perceived by patients as a punishment for their condition. Its negative image has much to do with previous poor applications performed by untrained practitioners.
- ECT is no more dangerous than minor surgery performed under general anaesthetic, with a death rate of approximately 1 in 10,000.

# Drug treatment

The prime treatment for schizophrenia is the use of antipsychotic drug therapy. The first antipsychotic was chlorpromazine, which was introduced in 1952 and very quickly had a major effect by enabling many schizophrenics to live relatively normal lives outside mental institutions. Chlorpromazine, in common with other antipsychotics, does not cure a patient of schizophrenia, but instead dampens symptoms down to a level where a fairly regular degree of functioning becomes possible.

Antipsychotics can be taken in tablet form, as a syrup or by injection, and can be divided into first generation (typical) and second generation (atypical) varieties. Typical varieties, such as chlorpromazine, work by arresting dopamine production through blocking the receptors in synapses that absorb dopamine, and thus reduce the positive symptoms of the disorder, such as auditory hallucinations. Atypical antipsychotics introduced in the 1990s, such as clozapine, work by acting upon serotonin as well as dopamine production systems and affect negative symptoms of the disorder, such as reduced emotional expression. Although atypical drugs are perceived as having fewer side effects, it is not always known specifically how they affect the brain to alleviate symptoms.

Some sufferers have to take a course of antipsychotics only once and will have no recurrence of the symptoms, while others have to take a regular dose in order to prevent their schizophrenic symptoms reappearing. There is also a sizeable minority of patients who do not really respond to drug treatment.

**Research**

- Kahn et al. (2008) compared first-generation with second-generation antipsychotics for effectiveness in treating first-instance schizophrenia, finding that, in general, antipsychotics are effective for at least 1 year, but that second-generation drugs are not necessarily any more effective than first-generation ones.
- Lieberman et al. (2005) examined the effectiveness of first- and second-generation antipsychotics in treating 1,432 chronic schizophrenics, finding that 74% of patients discontinued their treatment within 18 months due to intolerable side effects. Discontinuation rates and time to discontinuation were similar

### Knowledge check 10

What does research suggest about the effectiveness of drug therapies as a treatment for schizophrenia?

for first- and second-generation antipsychotics, though for different reasons: discontinuation of first-generation drugs was associated more with muscular disorders, while discontinuation of second-generation drugs was linked more to weight gain and metabolic effects.

- Davis et al. (1989) performed a meta-analysis of over 100 studies that compared antipsychotics with placebos, finding drugs to be more effective: more than 70% of sufferers treated with antipsychotics improved in condition after 6 weeks, while less than 25% improved with placebos, suggesting that antipsychotics do have a beneficial medical effect.

- Schooler et al. (2005), comparing the effectiveness of first- and second-generation antipsychotics, found both were effective in treating schizophrenia, with 75% of patients experiencing at least a 20% reduction in symptoms. However, 55% of those receiving a first-generation antipsychotic suffered relapses, compared to only 42% for a second-generation treatment, with relapses occurring earlier in those taking first-generation drug treatment. Side effects were also deemed to be lesser with second-generation antipsychotics. This implies second-generation drugs to be superior, but other studies have produced conflicting results.

## Evaluation

- Antipsychotics are a generally effective form of treatment, as they are relatively cheap to produce, are easy to administer and have a positive effect on many sufferers, allowing them to live relatively normal lives outside mental institutions.
- One problem with antipsychotics is the considerably high relapse rate, which can occur through not taking the medication regularly, or even when doing so.
- Antipsychotics can have serious side effects — for example, muscle tremors are associated with first-generation drugs. Second-generation antipsychotics were introduced as an attempt to reduce such problems, but there is evidence to suggest that these drugs can also incur serious side effects, such as a reduction in the number of white blood cells.
- Although the use of antipsychotics can produce relatively minor side effects, such as constipation and weight gain, some sufferers experience serious neurological symptoms that can lead to coma and death.

# Psychological therapies for schizophrenia

This section discusses the following psychological therapies for schizophrenia: behavioural therapy, psychodynamic therapy and cognitive behavioural therapy.

## Behavioural therapy

Behaviourism perceives mental disorders as maladaptive behaviours acquired through learning experiences, which can be eradicated and replaced with adaptive behaviours through behavioural therapies. Although there is little evidence that schizophrenia is actually a learned behaviour, some success in treating the disorder has been attained through the use of token economies, a behavioural therapy

### Examiner tip

When evaluating biological and psychological explanations of schizophrenia, a good way of accessing higher-level marks for evaluation is to refer to associated therapies. If therapies are supported by the findings of research in terms of their effectiveness, then this can be argued to support the theoretical foundations of the explanations they are based on.

**psychological therapies** treatments of schizophrenia through non-physiological methods of intervention

**behavioural therapies** treatments of schizophrenia that attempt to modify maladaptive behaviour by substituting new responses

technique in which a change in behaviour is achieved by means of tokens awarded for exhibiting desired actions. These reinforcers are provided immediately after a desired behaviour and then exchanged later for tangible goods or desired privileges, the technique being especially used with long-term institutional patients to prepare them for transfer into the community. The technique has proven successful in changing negative symptoms of schizophrenia, like poor motivation, poor attention and social withdrawal. This has the benefit that nursing staff subsequently view patients in a more positive way, which in itself has positive outcomes for the patients.

### Research

- McMonagle and Sultana (2000) conducted a review of token economy regimes over a 15-year period, finding that they did reduce negative symptoms, though it was unclear if the behavioural changes were maintained beyond the treatment programme.
- McReadie et al. (1978) assessed the use of token economies with male schizophrenics over a 6-month period, finding that patients who showed initiative and cooperated best with staff were the ones who benefited most from such a regime, which suggests that token economy is not an effective treatment for all sufferers.
- Upper and Newton (1971) found that weight gain, often associated with the use of antipsychotics, could be addressed with token economy regimes. Chronic schizophrenics reinforced with tokens and social approval were able to achieve a target of 3 pounds of body weight loss a week. However, the sample size was very small, making it difficult to generalise from the results.
- Ost et al. (1976) treated 12 chronic schizophrenics with a token economy regime for 8 months, finding positive changes in behaviour, such as a reduction in lip-biting. Of the five patients able to be discharged, none had been readmitted in the 1-year follow-up, suggesting that behavioural changes can be maintained after treatment ends.

### Examiner tip

In questions requiring an evaluation of a therapy (or an explanation of a disorder), take care to use research evidence to directly evaluate the therapy/explanation and not merely provide general methodological criticism of the study, for example that the study is an experiment and therefore shows causality, lacks ecological validity. Instead, say how it supports the therapy/explanation.

## Evaluation

- As changes in behaviour achieved through token economies tend not to continue when tokens are withdrawn, it would seem such treatments address the effects of schizophrenia rather than the causes.
- The positive changes attained through token economies may actually be due to other factors, such as the perception by nurses that it is they who are making progress and facilitating changes within their patients, which in turn gives them a positive view of patients and stimulates all concerned to strive for more progress.
- Glynn (1990) reports that, although token economy has a proven track record in treating the negative symptoms of schizophrenia, it has fallen out of fashion since the late 1970s, because of staff resistance, economic restraints, increased emphasis on community-based treatments, and legal and ethical challenges to its use.
- The focus of a token economy is on shaping and positively reinforcing desired behaviours and not on punishing undesirable behaviours.

# Psychodynamic therapy

Psychodynamic explanations of schizophrenia perceive the causes of schizophrenia as being rooted in early relationships and therefore psychodynamic therapy consists of providing insight to sufferers of the link between their symptoms and early experiences. Poor early relationships are seen as leading to a poor sense of self, which in turn can lead to schizophrenics having faulty metarepresentation and being unable to distinguish between their own thoughts and external sources. The therapist attempts to play a surrogate parenting role that facilitates normal personality development, thus allowing proper metarepresentation so that patients can distinguish their own thoughts from those of others.

psychodynamic therapy treatment of schizophrenia that aims to gain insight into the unconscious mind to reduce psychic tension

### Research

- Malmberg and Fenton (2009), in a review of psychodynamic therapies, found that such regimes have little, if any, benefit unless used in conjunction with drug treatments, suggesting that only with the use of antipsychotics can patients benefit from talking therapies.
- Normand and Bluestone (1986) found that combination treatments of antipsychotics and psychotherapy can be useful, but only for those patients with advanced verbal skills who are able to express themselves fully, suggesting that psychotherapy is not suitable as a universal treatment.
- Stein and Test (1980) found fewer symptoms, better social functioning and more patient satisfaction when home-treatment psychotherapy was used rather than hospital-based treatment, suggesting that institutionalisation may contribute to difficulties in treating schizophrenia.
- Knapp et al. (1994) found a programme of problem-orientated, home-based psychotherapy to be cost-effective, producing 'mildly encouraging' results over a 20-month period; this provides some support for psychotherapy.

### Knowledge check 11

What does research suggest about the effectiveness of (a) behavioural therapies and (b) psychodynamic therapies, as treatments for schizophrenia?

## Evaluation

- The use of psychodynamic therapies as a sole treatment for schizophrenia has, apart from several studies in the 1970s and 1980s, rarely been evaluated, so it is difficult to reach firm conclusions about such treatments.
- There is evidence that, rather than being helpful, psychotherapy can have adverse effects. Stone (1986) reported a high suicide rate among schizophrenics treated with psychotherapy, while Gunderson et al. (1984) found those receiving such treatment spent longer in hospital than those receiving other forms of treatment.
- Barton (1976) believes psychotherapy has an advantage over other treatments in that it can be administered outside of hospital, thus reducing the risk of institutionalisation.
- The theoretical basis for using psychodynamic therapies with schizophrenia is weak and there is little supporting evidence for its use, unless as a combination therapy with drug treatment therapy; there is no strong case for its use as a sole treatment.

# Cognitive behavioural therapy (CBT)

CBT has proved to be the main psychological treatment used to combat schizophrenia. The main idea behind the therapy is that beliefs, expectations and cognitive assessments of self, the environment and the nature of personal problems affect how a person perceives themselves and others, how problems are approached and how successful a person is in coping and attaining goals. As schizophrenia brings with it distorted perceptions, including those about the self, and disordered thinking, it seems reasonable to assume that CBT would be helpful in alleviating such symptoms, but only as long as antipsychotics are also used to reduce psychotic thought processes that interfere with psychological treatments.

Typically CBT is administered around once every 10 days, for about 12 sessions, to identify and alter irrational thinking. Drawings are often employed to display the links between a sufferer's thoughts, actions and emotions, with comprehension of where symptoms come from being very useful in reducing their anxiety levels.

## Research

- Rathod et al. (2005) found that non-Afro-Caribbean therapists had less success using CBT with Afro-Caribbean patients than with white patients, suggesting that the degree of empathy between clinicians and sufferers is important in determining the effectiveness of CBT.
- Turkington et al. (2006) assessed current practices and data concerning the use of CBT as a treatment for schizophrenia, concluding that CBT was highly effective and should be used as a mainstream treatment wherever possible.
- Trower et al. (2004) conducted a controlled trial of CBT, finding that it did not reduce in any way the intensity of hallucinations, but made them seem less of a threat by teaching sufferers that they 'outranked' the voices. Patients who received CBT had reductions of both positive and negative symptoms and a better quality of life. They concluded that CBT, though not a replacement for medication or suitable for everyone, can be a very effective treatment.
- Tarrier (2005) reviewed 20 controlled trials of CBT using 739 patients, finding persistent evidence of reduced symptoms, especially positive ones, lower relapse rates and a modest effect in speeding up the recovery rate of acutely ill patients. However, although CBT seemed effective in the short term, more research was needed to assess the therapy's long-term benefits.

## Evaluation

- A regime of CBT, combined with a course of antipsychotics, is considered to be the appropriate treatment strategy for schizophrenia in the UK and such a combination treatment is backed up by a considerable body of evidence.
- CBT was a relatively late addition to the treatments offered for schizophrenia, as scepticism was high due to the past failures of other individual psychotherapies.
- For CBT to be effective, training is essential, successful treatment being dependent upon developing empathy, respect, unconditional positive regard and honesty between patient and practitioner.

- CBT is not suitable for some patients, especially those who refuse medication or who are too thought-disorientated, too agitated, or too paranoid to form a trusting alliance with a practitioner.

**Summary**

- Schizophrenia affects thought processes and the ability to determine reality, divides into several subtypes and is diagnosed first by rank and then by additional symptoms.
- Reliability of diagnosis is quite high, but there are validity issues.
- Biological explanations include roles for genetics, evolution and biochemistry, as well as neuroanatomical and pregnancy factors.
- Psychological explanations focus on behaviourist learning experiences, as well as psychodynamic, cognitive and sociocultural factors.
- The two main biological treatments of schizophrenia are drug therapies involving antipsychotics, and ECT.
- Psychological treatments for schizophrenia include behavioural and psychodynamic therapies and the more favoured cognitive behavioural therapy (CBT).

# Depression

## Specification content

- *Clinical characteristics of the chosen disorder*
- *Issues surrounding the classification and diagnosis of the disorder, including reliability and validity*
- *Biological explanations of the disorder, for example genetics, biochemistry*
- *Psychological explanations of the disorder, for example behavioural, cognitive, psychodynamic and sociocultural*
- *Biological therapies for the disorder, including their evaluation in terms of appropriateness and effectiveness*
- *Psychological therapies for the disorder, for example behavioural, psychodynamic and cognitive behavioural, including their evaluation in terms of appropriateness and effectiveness*

There will be one optional question on depression on the examination paper. To ensure that you can answer it, you need to study and understand all the above.

Clinical characteristics refer to symptoms and types of depression that a sufferer may experience and you need a good working knowledge of these. Symptoms are listed within classification systems and you should also have a knowledge and understanding of issues of reliability (consistency) and validity (accuracy) associated with classifying and diagnosing depression.

Biological and psychological explanations are listed in the specification, so you need to cover both, though the specific explanations given (e.g. psychodynamic) are listed only as examples, meaning that they would not feature explicitly in any examination question. This also means that any other explanations, as long as they are biological or psychological, would be equally acceptable to study.

**depression** a mood disorder characterised by feelings of despondency and hopelessness

Finally, the specification focuses on biological and psychological therapies. Again the specific therapies referred to are listed only as examples, meaning that they cannot feature directly in any examination question and that any other therapies, as long as they are biological or psychological, would be equally acceptable to study. There is also a requirement to be able to evaluate both biological and psychological therapies in terms of how appropriate and effective they are.

# Clinical characteristics of depression

Depression is seen primarily as a mood disorder. There are two main types, unipolar depression and bipolar depression (also known as manic depression). It would be perfectly acceptable for examination purposes to study just one of these. Another way of subdividing depression distinguishes **endogenous depression**, which is related to internal biochemical and hormonal factors, and **reactive depression**, which is related to external environmental factors.

Up to 20% of people will suffer from depression at some time, with women being twice as vulnerable as men to developing the disorder. Depression can occur in cycles, with symptoms coming and going over time and generally lasting between 4 and 6 months, though it can be longer. Not only is depression a serious mental disorder in itself, but there is the additional problem of a high suicide rate associated with the condition, with 3.4% of severely depressed people committing suicide and about 60% of all suicides being associated with mood disorders.

DSM-IV lists the clinical characteristics of depression and the criteria state that at least five of the listed symptoms must be apparent every day for at least 2 weeks for depression to be diagnosed, with an impairment in general functioning also evident that cannot be accounted for by some other medical condition or event (such as mourning a loved one). Symptoms affect many aspects of functioning, including behavioural, motivational, somatic and emotional aspects. One of the five symptoms reported should be either a constant depressed mood or lessened interest in daily activities.

## Symptoms

The clinical symptoms are as follows:

(1) **constant depressed mood** — feelings of sadness either reported by the sufferer or observed by others
(2) **lessened interest** — diminished concern with and/or lack of pleasure in daily activities, either reported by the sufferer or observed by others
(3) **weight loss (or gain)** — significant decrease (or increase) in weight and/or appetite
(4) **sleep pattern disturbance** — constant insomnia or oversleeping
(5) **fatigue** — loss of energy and displacement of energy levels, for example becoming lethargic or agitated
(6) **reduced concentration** — difficulty in paying attention and/or slowed-down thinking and indecisiveness, either reported by the sufferer or observed by others
(7) **worthlessness** — constant feelings of reduced worth and/or inappropriate guilt
(8) **focus on death** — constant thoughts of death and/or suicide

---

**unipolar depression**
a form of depression that occurs without alternating periods of mania

**bipolar depression**
a form of depression characterised by alternating periods of depression and mania

---

**Knowledge check 13**

What requirements are necessary for a diagnosis of depression to be made?

---

**Examiner tip**

For questions asking for an outline of clinical characteristics of depression, use could be made not only of descriptions of clinical characteristics, but also of symptoms and subtypes, as these also can be considered to contain elements of clinical characteristics.

---

## Subtypes

Unipolar depression is also known as major depression and is differentiated from bipolar depression by the simple fact that it manifests itself purely as depression without the manic episodes that sufferers of bipolar depression experience. Unipolar depression is characterised by clinical symptoms, usually occurring in cycles over time.

Bipolar depression, also known as manic depression, typically involves several different types of episodes, including major depressive episodes, as with unipolar depression, and manic episodes where the sufferer is highly aroused, irritable or excited, full of energy, unable to sleep and often possessing an elevated sex drive. In the manic phase sufferers often display a significant increase in verbal communication, have trouble concentrating, become easily distracted, and display heightened goal-driven activity; they often simultaneously show an increase in self-esteem, experience a constant flight of ideas and thoughts, and become excessively involved in pleasurable but harmful activities, such as drug-taking.

Extreme manic episodes can lead to delusions and hallucinations. Most people experiencing mania also experience depressive episodes, though bipolar disorder can be diagnosed without evidence of depression. Between 1% and 2% of people will suffer from bipolar depression.

**Knowledge check 14**

Explain the difference between endogenous and reactive depression.

**Knowledge check 15**

Explain the difference between unipolar and bipolar depression.

# Issues surrounding the classification and diagnosis of depression

This section deals with issues of reliability and validity in relation to the classification and diagnosis of depression.

## Reliability

Reliability refers to the consistency of measurements and affects the classification and diagnosis of depression in two ways:

- **Test–retest reliability** occurs when a practitioner makes the same consistent diagnosis on separate occasions from the same information.
- **Inter-rater reliability** occurs when several practitioners make identical, independent diagnoses of the same patient.

Even with physical medical disorders, diagnoses are not always reliable, and making reliable diagnoses of depression is more problematic, as the practitioner uses mainly symptoms (what the patient reports) rather than physical signs to reach a decision. A major problem for diagnosis is that moods vary over time in most people, though the modern requirement for symptoms to be present for some time has aided the diagnostic process. Another problem is the need to consider the degree to which a person is depressed. Diagnosis was formerly carried out mainly by clinical interviews, but increasingly use has been made of depression inventories.

**reliability** the consistency of diagnosis

**Research**

- Einfeld et al. (2002) assessed the degree of inter-rater reliability between skilled clinicians in diagnosing depression, finding a high level of agreement that implies a high degree of inter-rater reliability.
- Moca (2007) found an 88% concordance rate for inter-rater reliability in the diagnosis of depression and a 78% concordance rate for test–retest reliability, lending support to the idea that diagnosis of depression is reliable.
- Baca-Garcia et al. (2007) reviewed the reliability of diagnosis of over 2,300 patients who were assessed at least ten times each, finding a concordance rate of only 55%, which suggests that reliability of diagnosis over time is relatively poor.
- Sato et al. (1996) assessed the test–retest reliability of the Inventory to Diagnose Depression, Lifetime Version (IDDL), finding a concordance rate of 77%, which implies that the use of inventories to diagnose depression is highly reliable.

**Knowledge check 16**

What has research suggested about the reliability of diagnosis of depression?

## Evaluation

- Beck (1972) evaluated the use of depression inventories, an alternative to psychiatric assessment by clinical interview, where a standard list of descriptive items is used in a uniform manner with all patients to facilitate diagnosis. This method of assessment is not subject to the inconsistencies and biases often found with psychiatric evaluations that occur through interview, and therefore can be used as a criterion measure by other clinicians. However, it often proved difficult for patients to discriminate between alternative descriptive statements, reducing the efficiency of such a diagnostic technique.
- A major problem in assessing the reliability of diagnosing depression over time is that patients may have improved in condition between diagnoses.
- Chao-Cheng et al. (2002) have raised the possibility of self-diagnosis of depression through the use of an internet-based self-assessment. The researchers reviewed the test–retest reliability of such a programme, finding a concordance rate of 75%, which suggests that it is a reliable method of diagnosis.
- Jürges (2008) reports that one problem with the use of self-assessment inventories to diagnose depression is that changes in self-ratings of health tend to be underestimated by patients, reducing the reliability of such a diagnostic method.

## Validity

**validity** the accuracy of diagnosis

Validity concerns how accurate, meaningful and useful diagnosis is. There are a number of ways in which validity can be assessed, for instance:

- **Reliability:** a valid diagnosis has first to be reliable (though reliability itself is no guarantee of validity).
- **Predictive validity:** if diagnosis leads to successful treatment, then the diagnosis can be seen as valid.
- **Descriptive validity:** for diagnosis to be valid, patients diagnosed with different disorders should actually differ from each other. Descriptive validity is reduced

by comorbidity, where patients are seen as having two or more disorders simultaneously, suggesting that such disorders are not actually separate from each other.

- **Aetiological validity:** for diagnosis to be valid, all patients diagnosed as depressed should have the same cause for their disorder.

### Research

- Van Weel-Baumgarten (2000) assessed the validity of diagnosis of depression by doctors in general practice in the Netherlands using DSM-IV criteria. There were 99 participants, of whom 33 were depressed, 33 had chronic nervous functional complaints and 33 had no mental disorders. Of the depressed participants 28 were (correctly) diagnosed as depressed, along with 7 of the participants with chronic nervous functional complaints, suggesting the validity of diagnosis to be high, although not perfect.
- Sanchez-Villegas et al. (2008) assessed the validity of the Structured Clinical Interview to diagnose depression, finding that 74.2% of those originally diagnosed as depressed had been accurately diagnosed, which suggests this diagnostic method is valid.
- Almeida and Almeida (1999) assessed the validity of the Geriatric Depression Scale (GDS) with both the ICD-10 and DSM-IV classification systems in diagnosing depression among 64 elderly Australians, finding the GDS to be highly valid, though not very useful in assessing the severity of depressive episodes.
- Zigler and Phillips (1961) reported that symptoms of depression were equally to be found in patients assessed as neurotic as in those assessed as having bipolar disorder, as well as in 25% of diagnosed schizophrenics, implying low diagnostic validity of depression.

## Evaluation

- Not all diagnostic scales in clinical use have been found to be valid. Anderson et al. (2003) used the previously proven valid GDS to assess the value of the Minimum Data Set Depression Rating Scale (MDSDRS), finding it to be of low validity and therefore of little clinical use.
- A significant obstacle to the treatment of depression is the failure to diagnose symptoms. Burrows et al. (1995) found healthcare providers under-diagnose depression in as much as 56% of nursing home residents.
- Validation of diagnostic scales is important not only in proving such criteria to be valid in themselves, but because such diagnostic scales can then be used to further assess the validity of other diagnostic measures.
- Although the classification and diagnosis of depression are not without criticisms, they are probably the most effective method of assessment and diagnostic criteria and allow clinicians to communicate using a common language.

### Examiner tip

Students often get the relationship between reliability and validity confused. A valid diagnosis must be reliable (consistent), but a reliable diagnosis does not guarantee validity (accuracy). For example, adding 1 + 1 several times and always getting the answer 3 is reliable but is not valid. Adding up 1 + 1 several times and always getting 2 is, however, both reliable and valid.

### Knowledge check 17

What has research indicated about the validity of diagnosis of depression?

# Biological explanations of depression

**biological explanations**
depression perceived as
having a physiological cause

**Biological explanations** have focused on several areas, including genetics, evolution and the biochemical influences of hormones and neurotransmitters. A variety of indicators suggests biology underpins depression, including hereditary factors; the uniformity of symptoms across genders, age groups and cultural groups; the physical aspects of symptoms, such as weight fluctuations and fatigue; and the fact that biological therapies such as drug treatments have been successful in addressing the symptoms of depression. Overall, evidence does indicate a major contributory role for biological factors, though environmental factors also seem to be involved in the onset of depression.

## Genetic explanations

**genetic explanations**
depression perceived
as transmitted through
hereditary means

Research has traditionally used twin, family and adoption studies to assess what role, if any, **genetic explanations** might play in the causation of depression. Results from all sources indicate depression to have a genetic component, though one of the problems with such studies is separating out environmental influences: for instance, it is known that children of depressed parents are more likely to develop the disorder than children of non-depressed parents, but does this indicate a genetic link or an environmental one?

More recently, technology has advanced, allowing gene mapping studies to be undertaken. This entails comparing genetic material from families with a high incidence of depression and families with a low incidence of the disorder. Results from gene mapping indicate that several genes rather than just one gene are probably involved, and that what genes do is make some individuals more vulnerable than others to developing the disorder. Therefore genes probably do not cause depression on their own; indeed, if they did, the concordance rate between MZ (monozygotic or identical) twins would be 100%, which it clearly is not.

> **Research**
> - Sevey et al. (2000) reviewed twin studies of bipolar disorder, finding a concordance rate of 69.3% in MZ (identical) twins, but only 20% in DZ (dizygotic or non-identical) twins. As MZ twins share 100% genetic similarity compared to 50% in DZ twins, this suggests a genetic influence on bipolar disorder.
> - Kendler et al. (2006) investigated whether genetic influences for depression were greater in Swedish females than males. A meta-analysis of five twin studies incorporating 42,161 twins (including 15,493 complete pairs) was conducted and heritability was found to be higher in females than males, 42% compared to 29%, suggesting that genetic risk factors are higher for women.
> - Wender et al. (1986) found that adopted children who develop depression are more likely to have a biological parent with the disorder even though they are raised in a different environment, implying biological factors to be more influential than environmental ones.

- Mendlewicz and Rainer (1977) performed an adoption study focusing on adoptees with bipolar disorder, finding the rate of the disorder to be 7% in biological parents, compared to 0% in adoptive parents, suggesting a stronger genetic influence.
- Taylor et al. (1995) reviewed family studies of depression and found the prevalence of the disorder in the general population to be 1%, while in first-degree relatives of a bipolar depressive it was between 5% and 10%, implying a clear genetic pathway to bipolar disorder.
- Oruc et al. (1998) found that depression often occurs across generations in families and the chances of developing the disorder increase the closer the genetic relationship is. First-degree relatives of those diagnosed with depression are up to three times more likely to develop the disorder than others.
- Caspi et al. (2005) used gene mapping to find a relationship between depression and abnormalities in the 5-HTT gene, suggesting a genetic link. As 5-HTT is associated with the manufacture of serotonin, this also implies a link between genetics and biochemical factors.
- Wilhelm et al. (2006) found that individuals who experienced negative life events and had the short-short variation of the serotonin transporter gene were more likely to become depressed, suggesting that this variation of the transporter gene makes people more vulnerable to developing depression in the presence of negative life events.

**Examiner tip**

When revising material for the psychopathology section of your Unit 4 examination, ensure that you have prepared material for both a short and a longer version of answers requiring an outline. Sometimes an outline may be worth just 4 marks but, at other times, 8 marks. A different amount of material would therefore be required for these questions.

## Evaluation

- With twin studies there is a possibility of diagnostic unreliability, where the researcher is biased in making a diagnosis of one twin while having full knowledge of the psychiatric status of the other twin (i.e. if a researcher is aware that one twin is depressive, this may cloud their judgement in assessing whether the other twin is depressive too).
- Twin and family studies often suggest a genetic factor in the onset of depression, but such studies often do not consider the influence of social class and socio-psychological factors on family members.
- Sullivan et al. (2000) reported that the few adoption studies of depression that have been carried out have been negatively affected by methodological flaws, such as small sample sizes and indirect methods of clinical diagnosis, making it difficult to draw clear conclusions.
- Gene mapping offers the possibility of developing tests to identify people with a high risk of developing depression, though this could raise a wide range of socially sensitive and ethical concerns.
- Although family studies tend to support the genetic viewpoint, they often fail to consider shared environmental influences, lessening support for a genetic explanation.
- Overall, the findings from studies involving genetics suggest strong evidence for the **diathesis–stress model**, where individuals inherit different levels of genetic predisposition to developing depression, but ultimately it is environmental triggers that determine if an individual actually goes on to develop the disorder.

# Evolutionary explanations

Several evolutionary explanations of depression have been proposed, on the basis that, as the disorder continues to be represented in the gene pool, it must serve an adaptive function and therefore have a survival value.

The **rank theory** (Price 2004) is part of the **social competition hypothesis** and states that, if an individual is clearly losing a dominance fight within a social group, then depression serves the useful function of getting the individual to admit defeat, accept a more submissive role and thus be protected from further harm. Therefore clinical depression is the pathological result of an adaptive emotional mechanism that allows people to perceive whether they are trying to reach unattainable goals and persuades them to stop before incurring injury.

The **genome lag theory** proposes that the conditions in our evolutionary past (the 'environment of evolutionary adaptedness' or EEA) that caused depression to be beneficial, as stated by rank theory, do not apply in the modern world, so that depression often is not the best solution to modern-day problems, such as relationship breakdowns. In other words, depression was an adaptive solution to problems in our evolutionary past and is still present as an inherited tendency even though it is mostly maladaptive nowadays.

The **social navigation theory** (Watson and Andrews 2002) states that depression evolved to solve cognitively complex social problems that are resistant to conventional social negotiation. Depression is seen as emanating from conflict between where we are and where we wish to be; the sobering quality of depression makes us aware of changes that need to occur in our social network, causing us to slow down and think more systematically to help us formulate strategies that allow us to reach our goals. Depression is also seen as providing an honest signal of need, motivating close social partners to provide support and help as the depression has negative implications for their inclusive fitness (i.e. 'help me or you will lose out too').

**evolutionary explanations** depression perceived as possessing an adaptive value linked to survival

**Examiner tip**

When describing biological explanations of depression, such as the evolutionary explanation, it may be necessary to outline the explanation in general, for example that evolutionary explanations see an adaptive advantage to human qualities and behaviours. However, answers that are not specifically oriented at explaining how evolutionary theory views depression will earn little, if any, credit.

**Research**

- Shively et al. (2006), using PET scans, found that high-ranking monkeys had serotonin levels twice as high as other monkeys; that serotonin levels fell if monkeys lost rank; and that monkeys gained rank if given supplementary serotonin. The findings support rank theory.
- Price (1987) states that unipolar depression from the internal inhibitory process has benefits for an individual in preventing further damage and for the group in stopping conflicts, while it also explains bipolar disorder, in that when an individual gains rank they experience elation (mania).
- Crawford (2005) believes the genome lag theory is not supported, as the differences between the modern world and the EEA have been exaggerated and they actually share many similarities.
- Buss (1996) believes we are more exposed to highly attractive people in the media than we were in the EEA, which can lead to feelings of inadequacy and thus depression, lending support to the genome lag theory.

- Hartlage et al. (1993) found that depressives under-performed on cognitively demanding tasks, such as memory tasks, because their efforts were more focused or committed elsewhere, supporting the social navigation theory.
- Hawton and Fagg (1992) found that suicide attempts of depressed individuals stop when their relationships with close social partners improve, supporting the social navigation theory.

**Knowledge check 18**
How do the following biological explanations perceive the causes of depression: (a) genetic explanations; (b) evolutionary explanations?

## Evaluation

- It is not clear if serotonin is a cause or an effect of changes in social rank and also there is a difficulty in generalising findings from research with monkeys to humans.
- Price and Sloman (1987) believe that rank theory can explain how depression evolved, through the **yielding subroutine**, where the submissive component of ritual agonistic conflict allowed social harmony to be restored, and the **winning subroutine**, where mania evolved as the victorious component of such social conflicts.
- In more developed countries where there is a bigger difference between modern culture and the EEA, depression rates are higher, supporting the idea that genome lag is a contributory factor to developing depression.
- Genome lag theory can explain why depression still occurs, because human culture has evolved without our genes evolving and therefore we experience 'stone age' processes in a 'space age' world.
- Watson (2008) believes the social navigation theory shows how depression is adaptive, in that it allows the formation of solutions that reduce the chances of suicide.
- Strassman and Dunbar (1990) argue that depression may be the result of the modern-day breakdown of the close-knit nuclear family that provided strong kin support, thereby endorsing the social navigation theory.

## Biochemical explanations

Biochemical explanations are centred upon the idea that abnormal levels of neurotransmitters and hormones cause depression. Attention has especially centred upon a group of neurotransmitters called monoamines, such as serotonin, noradrenaline and dopamine, low levels of which have been found in the brains of depressives. The importance of monoamines is supported by the fact that antidepressant drugs work by increasing the production of monoamines.

Certain forms of depression, such as premenstrual syndrome (PMS), seasonal affective disorder (SAD) and post-natal depression, have also been associated with hormonal changes.

biochemical explanations depression perceived as determined through the actions of neurotransmitters and hormones

**Examiner tip**

An excellent way of producing high-quality answers to questions on explanations of depression is to illustrate how factors can be combined. For example, with biochemical explanations, the neurotransmitter noradrenaline can be offered as a sole explanation but can also be combined with the fact that abnormal brain structures may affect levels of noradrenaline that then lead to depression.

**Knowledge check 19**

How does the biochemical explanation perceive the cause of depression?

**Research**

- McNeal and Cimbolic (1986) found low amounts of the chemical 5-H1AA (created when serotonin is broken down) in the cerebrospinal fluid of depressives, supporting the biochemical explanation.
- Mann et al. (1996) found major depression results from either a deficiency of serotonin, or insufficient serotonin receptors, suggesting a biochemical cause to depression.
- Delack et al. (1995) found that fluoxetine, a selective serotonin reuptake inhibitor (SSRI), was effective in addressing the symptoms of depression, lending support to the biochemical explanation.
- Mann et al. (1996) found that the reduction in depressive symptoms achieved by increasing monoamine levels through the usage of antidepressants is reversed when serotonin levels are decreased by dietary manipulation, providing evidence for the biochemical explanation.
- Teuting et al. (1981) found abnormally low amounts of by-products associated with noradrenaline levels in urine samples from depressives, implying a biochemical cause for the disorder.
- Zhou et al. (2005) found that SSRIs work by increasing dopamine levels in depressives, suggesting a role for this neurotransmitter in the causation of depression.
- Kalynchuck et al. (2005) reported that patients with Cushing disease are often depressed and have high levels of the stress hormone cortisol, suggesting depression stems from chronic over-stimulation of the hypothalamic–pituitary–adrenal axis, which produces the hormone.
- Chen et al. (2006) reported that a decline in the level of the hormone insulin following childbirth might be responsible for post-natal depression. Insulin affects the secretion of serotonin in the brain, therefore decreased insulin may be influencing depression.

## Evaluation

- An underlying problem with the biochemical explanation is the question of whether such fluctuations in neurotransmitter and hormonal levels are a cause or an effect of depression.
- Klimek et al. (1997) performed post-mortems on depressives and non-depressives, finding differences in the structure of the locus coeruleus, a brain area associated with the production of noradrenaline, suggesting that abnormal brain structures may affect neurotransmitter levels, which leads to depression.
- The fact that monoamine neurotransmitters are usually involved in arousal and mood levels points towards them being involved in depression, which is classed as a mood disorder.
- Antidepressant drugs do not produce the same effects in all depressives, suggesting that causes may be different for different individuals.
- Neurotransmitter levels are affected immediately by taking antidepressants, but symptoms often take weeks to improve, suggesting a lack of support for the biochemical viewpoint.

- The fact that women are more subject than men to fluctuating hormone levels, such as with menstruation, pregnancy and the menopause, may explain why women are up to three times more likely than men to suffer from depression in their lifetime.
- As reduced insulin levels have been associated with post-natal depression, it may be possible to prevent the disorder by increasing the amount of carbohydrates eaten, as carbohydrates stimulate the production of insulin.

# Psychological explanations of depression

Although evidence indicates that biological factors play an important role in the onset of depression, it is generally accepted that psychological factors are also involved. There are several psychological explanations of depression, including the behaviourist, psychodynamic, cognitive and sociocultural explanations.

## Behaviourist explanations

Behaviourist explanations see depression as a learned condition and therefore do not perceive the disorder as a mental illness with a physical cause.

Lewinsohn (1974) proposed that the disorder occurs due to a **decline in positive reinforcement**. For example, after a romantic relationship ends there are reduced opportunities of experiencing enjoyable outcomes and thus fewer positive reinforcements, resulting in depression. The affected individual may become caught in a cycle of social withdrawal, which prolongs the depression.

Operant conditioning can explain depressive behaviour as being rewarding due to the attention and sympathy it brings, reinforcing such behaviour as a secondary gain. Behaviourism can also explain the tendency of depression to run in families in social learning terms, as being merely a result of observing and imitating affected family members.

Another way in which behaviourism can explain depression is through learned helplessness, where individuals learn through experience that they seemingly cannot influence events (for instance being unemployed and applying for many jobs but not even getting one interview), and this leads to a chronic loss of motivation and eventually depression.

**Research**
- Maier and Seligman (1976) found that participants placed in a situation where escape from noise or shocks was impossible did not try to escape from later similar situations where escape was possible, lending support to the idea of learned helplessness.
- Coleman (1986) found that individuals who receive a low rate of positive reinforcement for their social behaviours become increasingly passive and non-responsive, leading to a depressive mood, which provides support for Lewinsohn's learning theory.

**psychological explanations** depression perceived as having non-physiological causes

**behaviourist explanations** depression perceived as determined through learning processes

**Examiner tip**

With 24-mark questions requiring an outline and an evaluation (e.g. 'Outline and evaluate explanations of depression'), students can spend too long on the outline, leaving little time for evaluation. The outline is worth only 8 marks whereas the evaluation is worth 16 marks, so only one-third of the time should be spent on the outline and two-thirds on the evaluation.

- Rehm (1977) found that depressed individuals had deficits in self-regulatory monitoring, and proposed a behavioural model for the self-control of depression that focused upon an individual's maladaptive self-regulatory processes in coping with stress.
- Rice and McLaughlin (2001) found that depressive individuals tend to focus upon negative events, set overly stringent criteria for evaluating their performance and administer little reinforcement to themselves, supporting Lewinsohn's model, as it focuses on the idea that reduced activity and lack of reinforcement are correlated to helplessness and depression.

## Evaluation

- Although behaviourism can explain depression in terms of secondary gain, for example the sympathetic attention of others following a negative event, it cannot explain why depression continues after such attention has declined.
- Kanter et al. (2004) state that behaviour analysis has yet to offer an account of depression that satisfactorily addresses its complexity.
- Ferster (1973) demonstrated that reinforcement schedules and environmental influences were important factors in depressive behaviour, which created opportunities to develop specific behavioural techniques for treatment of the disorder.
- Learned helplessness has not proven to be a universal occurrence, as in some cases where individuals were placed in situations of helplessness the experience actually led to improved performance.

## Psychodynamic explanation

**psychodynamic explanation** depression seen as rooted in childhood experiences of loss or rejection

Freud's (1917) psychodynamic explanation saw depression as related to childhood melancholic experiences of loss or rejection within the family and that depression in adulthood was a type of delayed regret for this loss. A child would experience anger over such loss or rejection, but not being able to express this anger would repress it, directing it inwards and lowering self-esteem. Similar loss or rejection in adult life was also seen as driving a person to re-experience their childhood loss.

Similarly, Bowlby (1973) proposed that experiencing separation from a mother figure in early childhood could lead to an enhanced vulnerability to depression in later life.

**Research**

- Abela et al. (2007) gave 79 children questionnaires assessing self-criticism, dependency and depressive symptoms, and found that children high in dependency exhibited no increases in hopelessness or depression symptoms following negative life events, reducing support for the psychodynamic explanation.
- Swaffer and Hollin (2001) gave questionnaires to young offenders, finding that those who repressed anger had an increased vulnerability to developing depression, supporting the psychodynamic model.

- Harlow et al. (1965) separated baby monkeys from their mothers at birth and found they exhibited symptoms of depression, in line with the psychodynamic model.
- Bemporad (1992) found that individuals whose needs were not met, or were excessively met, in the first 18 months of life tended to spend their lives searching for love and approval, causing a greater impact of loss when a loved one died and leading to clinical depression, which lends support to the psychodynamic theory.

**Knowledge check 20**
How do the following psychological explanations perceive the causes of depression: (a) behaviourist explanations; (b) psychodynamic explanations?

## Evaluation

- The psychodynamic theory can explain the physical factors of depression as well as psychological ones. For instance, the lack of energy often associated with depression is seen as due to the amount of energy expended in keeping anger repressed.
- There is a problem with evidence gained from animal studies, such as Harlow's separated monkeys study, as it cannot necessarily be extrapolated to humans.
- Psychodynamic theory is difficult to scientifically test and thus it is often difficult to refute or provide support for.
- Psychodynamic explanations have parallels with more modern theories of cognitive vulnerability to depression, which also perceive a link with experiences of loss.

**Examiner tip**
IDA points are not an essential requirement for Unit 4 answers but relevant points concerning issues, debates and approaches (IDA) can help form excellent evaluative points. For example, when evaluating the psychodynamic explanation of depression, reference could be made to the non-falsifiable nature of the psychodynamic approach.

# Cognitive explanations

Beck's (1976) cognitive explanation believed that, rather than having a negative viewpoint due to being depressed, people actually become depressed by having dysfunctional beliefs about themselves. Beck explained depression as resulting from three types of negative thought patterns:

**cognitive explanation**
depression perceived as determined through maladaptive thought patterns

(1) **Negative automatic thinking** — involving the negative cognitive triad, which regards negative thoughts as being about:
  (a) **the self** — where individuals regard themselves as being helpless, worthless and inadequate
  (b) **the world** — where obstacles are perceived within one's environment that cannot be dealt with
  (c) **the future** — where personal worthlessness is seen as hindering any improvements
  These components of the negative cognitive triad are perceived as self-defeating and resulting in depression.
(2) **Selective attention to the negative** — involves paying attention to the negative aspects, and thus ignoring the positive ones, of a given situation, culminating in reaching negative conclusions.
(3) **Negative self-schemas** — involves possessing a set of negative self-beliefs, acquired through parental criticism, which in turn influences an individual's perception of future situations in a negative fashion.

Overall, therefore, depression is seen as resulting from cognitive vulnerabilities.

Abramson et al. (1978) outlined another cognitive explanation, in terms of attributional style, which involves linking learned helplessness to depression. Depressives are perceived as attributing failures to themselves rather than to external factors, with such attributions being regarded as stable and universal rather than specific. Abramson et al. (1989) also proposed attributional style to be involved in hopelessness theory, whereby individuals with a negative attributional style as well as hopelessness (a belief that negative events will occur) are likely to develop depression.

**Research**

- Boury et al. (2001) monitored students' negative thoughts with the Beck Depression Inventory (BDI), and found that depressed individuals misinterpret facts and experiences in a negative fashion and feel hopeless about the future, giving support to Beck's cognitive explanation.
- Saisto et al. (2001) studied expectant mothers, and found an increase in depressive symptoms in those who did not adjust personal goals to match the specific demands of the transition to motherhood but indulged instead in negative thinking patterns, supporting Beck's cognitive theory.
- McIntosh and Fischer (2000) tested the negative cognitive triad to see if it actually contains three distinct types of negative thought, and found no clear separation of negative thoughts but instead a single, one-dimensional negative perception of the self. This suggests that retention of all three areas of the triad as separate dimensions is unnecessary for representing the structure of depressive cognition.
- Seligman (1974) reported that students who made global, stable attributions remained depressed for longer after examinations, supporting the cognitive explanation in terms of attributional style.

## Evaluation

- There is a wealth of research evidence supporting a link between cognitive vulnerability and the onset of depression, with depressives selectively attending to negative stimuli.
- The cognitive explanation of depression lends itself readily to scientific research, allowing refinement of cognitive models to promote greater understanding of the disorder.
- A relatively high degree of success has been achieved in treating depression with therapies based on cognitive explanations, thus providing support for such explanations.
- The majority of evidence linking negative thinking to depression is correlational and thus does not show that negative thoughts cause depression.

## Sociocultural explanations

sociocultural
explanations depression
perceived as determined
through family and social
environments

Sociocultural explanations are based upon social and cultural factors, such as the family and social environments. Such explanations have focused on the impact that life events, in the form of stressors, can have on the onset and maintenance of depression. For instance, they consider whether individuals who become depressed have experienced high levels of life event stressors in the period preceding the onset of the disorder.

There has also been focus on the role played by social networks, especially on whether people with reduced social support are more vulnerable to becoming depressed and staying depressed for prolonged periods. There is a possible link here between the level of social and interpersonal skills that individuals possess and the likelihood of becoming depressed.

### Research

- Leavey et al. (2007) examined the strong tendency of Irish migrants to Britain to become depressed by conducting interviews with such migrants living in London. They found that depression often had origins in difficult life events and circumstances, supporting the sociocultural viewpoint.
- Cox (2007) examined sociocultural aspects of post-natal depression (PND) in East Africa, and found that mothers who did not take part in traditional post-natal rituals experienced reduced self-esteem and stressful marital relationships, leading to ambivalent social status and increased risk of experiencing PND. The findings support the sociocultural explanation.
- Takaaki (2003) reported that the incidence of unipolar depression in Japan had increased dramatically and that this could be linked to changes in family and social environments. These changes include the movement of younger people to urban environments and the collapse of traditional family structures, leading to an increase in stressful life events and a lack of family support to deal with such stressors. This fits the sociocultural explanation of depression.
- Rodgers et al. (2009) gave self-report questionnaires to 509 adolescents, assessing levels of depression, body dissatisfaction, bulimic tendencies and sociocultural influences on physical appearance. They found that males and females who displayed high levels of depressive symptoms perceived stronger media and peer influences on physical appearance, again providing support for the sociocultural viewpoint.

### Knowledge check 21

How do the following psychological explanations perceive the causes of depression: (a) cognitive explanations; (b) sociocultural explanations?

## Evaluation

- The highly regarded **diathesis–stress model** can be seen as part of the life events approach, in that it considers the chances of an individual becoming depressed to be linked not only to the degree of genetic vulnerability but also to the number and severity of stressful life events experienced.
- Although research tends to support a role for sociocultural factors in the onset and maintenance of depression, poor interpersonal and social skills could be an effect of being depressed rather than a cause.
- A strength of the sociocultural viewpoint is that it can explain differences in prevalence rates between ethnic, gender and socioeconomic groups — explaining, for instance, that women are more likely to develop depression because they are subject to more life event stressors than men.
- Although research tends to indicate the importance of sociocultural factors in the development of depression, evidence from other sources, such as that on biological factors, suggests they are not generally the only cause of onset.

# Biological therapies for depression

The two common biological therapies for depression are drugs (chemotherapy) and electro-convulsive therapy (ECT), with psychosurgery also used in a very few severe cases where sufferers do not respond to other forms of treatment and are at high risk of death by suicide. Seasonal affective disorder (SAD), a specific form of depression generally occurring in the dark winter months, has also been successfully treated with light therapy, involving the use of very bright full-spectrum lights at particular times of day. This treatment is often used in conjunction with drugs.

## Drug treatment

The most common treatments for depression are antidepressant drug therapies, which generally stimulate the production of monoamine neurotransmitters in the brain, leading to increased physical arousal. In Britain more than £291 million was spent on antidepressants in 2006.

Old-fashioned antidepressants such as monoamine oxidase inhibitors (MAOIs) stop serotonin, noradrenaline and dopamine being broken down so that their levels are increased, while tricyclics stop serotonin and noradrenaline being reabsorbed so that again levels are increased. Although effective in treating the symptoms of depression, these antidepressants can cause side effects, such as drowsiness and constipation. More modern antidepressants tend to affect the level of only one monoamine: for instance, selective serotonin reuptake inhibitors (SSRIs), such as Prozac, prevent serotonin being reabsorbed or broken down. There is no one best drug, as patients tend to respond differently to different drugs and drug choice can also be affected by symptoms displayed and any side effects exhibited.

**Research**

- Olfson et al. (2006) found antidepressant drug treatment for depression was related to a high incidence of suicide attempts in children and adolescents between 6 and 18 years of age. These findings support careful clinical monitoring during antidepressant drug treatment of severely depressed young people.
- David et al. (2009) performed research with rodents, finding that SSRIs reverse changes in the hippocampus caused by depression. The researchers went on to identify student genes whose expression was decreased in the hypothalamus and normalised by Prozac. Mice deficient in the gene beta-arrestin 2 displayed a reduced response to Prozac, indicating that beta-arrestin 2 signalling is necessary for the antidepressant effects of Prozac to occur.
- Kirsch (2008) found that the new generation of antidepressants, such as SSRIs, work no better than a placebo for most patients with mild and even severe forms of depression, and accused drug companies of suppressing research evidence that cast doubt on these drugs' effectiveness.
- Furukawa et al. (2003) reviewed 35 studies, finding antidepressants to be more effective than placebos, which suggests antidepressants can be an appropriate treatment for depression.

## Evaluation

- Akira et al. (2009) reported that recent research has highlighted an association between cytokines and depression that suggests cytokine-based antidepressant drugs may increase the effectiveness of drug treatment for the disorder.
- Antidepressant drugs are very cost-effective, are available in tablet form (a familiar and trusted form of treatment), and have the added benefit of being self-administered.
- Research indicates placebo effects of drug treatment to be high, suggesting a psychological rather than biological effect.
- Research indicates psychological treatments to be more effective than antidepressants, but such treatments tend not to be favoured as they are more costly.

# ECT

ECT (electro-convulsive therapy) was originally introduced as a treatment for schizophrenia by Cerletti (1935), but quickly became a standard treatment for depression. ECT produces a seizure that lasts up to a minute. Bilateral shocks (given to both sides of the head) are seen as being more effective than unilateral shocks (given to just one side of the head) but can also produce more side effects. Modern forms of ECT use mild shocks given for very brief periods and ECT is generally administered to a patient two to three times a week for about eight treatments, along with an anaesthetic and a muscle relaxant to prevent bone fractures.

ECT has proved to be a controversial treatment; it can seem brutal and has serious side effects such as temporary memory loss, which can get more severe as treatments continue. It is also not completely clear how the treatment works. However, modern forms are more humane and are deemed to be an appropriate treatment when other treatments have failed, or when a patient is perceived as a high suicide risk.

### Research

- Paguin et al. (2008) performed a meta-analysis of ECT that compared studies of ECT, placebos and antidepressant drugs, and found a significant superiority of ECT in all comparisons, suggesting ECT to be a valid therapeutic tool for treating depression, including severe and resistant forms.
- Levy (1968) compared bilateral with unilateral forms of ECT, finding that unilateral treatments caused less memory loss, but bilateral treatments produced slightly better relief of depressive symptoms.
- Antunes et al. (2009) reviewed studies on the effectiveness of ECT, symptom remission, patients' perceptions, cognitive impairments and quality of life. They found that ECT was more effective than antidepressants, remission rates were between 50% and 80%, quality of life improved and patients had a positive perception of the treatment. The findings suggest that ECT remains a highly appropriate treatment, especially since the introduction of improvements in procedure.
- Taylor (2007) reported that ECT produces a response rate of up to 55% in depressives and a response rate of between 80% and 90% when ECT is used as initial treatment for severe depression.

**ECT (electro-convulsive therapy)** treatment of depression by applying electrical voltages across the brain

### Examiner tip
When evaluating therapies, it is creditworthy to comment on ethical considerations. For example, are depressives, in their mentally disordered state, truly able to give informed consent to receive ECT? An elaboration of this point could refer to a cost–benefit analysis, for instance the lack of informed consent considered against the fact that treatment may prevent depressives from committing suicide.

### Knowledge check 23
What does research suggest about the effectiveness of ECT as a treatment for depression?

## Evaluation

- The side effects of ECT seem to be more severe with children, adolescents, the elderly and pregnant women, so ECT should not be used as a treatment for these categories of people, unless as a last resort.
- Use of ECT declined in the USA between 1975 and 1986 from 58,667 to 36,558 patients due to the introduction of new generation antidepressants and to negative media reports. However, from 1987 to 1992 the use of ECT rose from 4.2 to 5.1 per 10,000 individuals, suggesting that the treatment is now seen in a more favourable light and that the new generation antidepressants have not been as effective as originally hoped.
- Coffey (1998) states that patients should be fully evaluated using a set of criteria before ECT is prescribed. This should include a review of previous psychiatric history, a medical evaluation to define risk factors, the gaining of informed consent, appropriate diagnostic tests and a review of any previous ECT treatments.
- Apart from side effects such as memory loss, another serious problem with ECT is the high relapse rate associated with the treatment. Sackheim et al. (2001) reported that 84% of patients relapsed within 6 months, implying the treatment not to be effective in the long term.

# Psychological therapies for depression

This section discusses the following psychological therapies for depression: behavioural therapies, psychodynamic therapies and cognitive behavioural therapy.

## Behavioural therapies

Behaviourism perceives mental disorders as maladaptive behaviours acquired through learning experiences, which can be eradicated and replaced with adaptive behaviours through behavioural therapies. Therefore behaviourist treatments are based upon the idea that depression is a learned behaviour that can be addressed by using learning theory principles, such as operant conditioning and social learning. Reinforcements are used to elevate mood and encourage participation in positive behaviours. Social reinforcement, from family members and social networks, is also utilised to provide support for the depressed individual.

**Behavioural activation therapy** (BAT) is a powerful and progressive therapy that avoids the idea that depression is an illness or weakness and instead perceives the disorder as an indication of the things in an individual's life that need to change. Exercises are used that help depressives to concentrate on activities that bring feelings of joy and mastery. A schedule of activities is built up that a sufferer needs to participate in to create a normal and satisfying life. The therapy offers quick relief from depression, as it connects patients with simple, naturally occurring reinforcements in order to change how they approach day-to-day activities, make life choices and deal with crises.

**Social skills training** (SST) is a form of behaviour therapy used to help people who have difficulties in relating to other people, as is often the case with depressives.

psychological therapies treatments of depression based on non-physiological means of intervention

behavioural therapies treatments of depression that attempt to modify maladaptive behaviour by the substitution of new responses

Those lacking certain social skills can have difficulties in building a network of supportive friends and become more and more socially isolated, increasing the risk of becoming depressive. SST operates on the principle that when patients improve their social skills then their levels of self-esteem will rise and others will respond more favourably to them. A key goal of the therapy is to improve a patient's ability to function in everyday social situations. Patients are taught to alter behaviour patterns by practising selected behaviours in individual or group therapy sessions.

### Research

- Houghton et al. (2008) evaluated the effectiveness of BAT on 42 patients with self-reported depression, finding that the treatment was effective and tolerable, with a low drop-out rate.
- De Jong-Meyer and Hautzinger (1996) assessed 'Coping with Depression', a course of group therapy treatment based upon BAT, and found that it achieved comparable acute outcome to and better long-term outcome than antidepressant medication, indicating that the therapy provides clinicians with a convenient, cost-effective treatment that can be tailored to the individual needs of patients.
- Herson et al. (1984) reported that social skills treatments are equal in effectiveness to traditional psychotherapies in addressing the symptoms of depression.
- La Fromboise and Rowe (1983) found that **structured learning therapy**, a treatment based on SST, is more readily employable for different groups of patients than traditional psychotherapies, and has helped improve the psychosocial functioning of males and females of varying age groups and ethnic backgrounds, as well as proving useful in treating those who have difficulties with traditional psychotherapy.

**Examiner tip**
In questions requiring an evaluation of a therapy (or an explanation of a disorder), take care to use research evidence to directly evaluate the therapy/explanation and not merely provide general methodological criticism of the study, for example that the study is an experiment and therefore shows causality, lacks ecological validity. Instead, say how it supports the therapy/explanation.

## Evaluation

- BAT is a useful treatment for depression, as it can be successfully modified for use with different groups of patients who have very different needs, such as the elderly or adolescents.
- BAT compares favourably with cognitive behavioural therapy (CBT), producing a similar success rate of 50% immediately after treatment, reducing to 25% after 2 years. As BAT is a simpler method of treatment it can therefore be argued to be more effective than CBT.
- Therapists using SST should progress slowly, so that patients are not overwhelmed by attempting to change too many behaviours at one time, which may intensify their feelings of social incompetence and deepen their depression rather than reduce it.
- One problem with SST is the difficulty in generalising newly learned social skills to real-life situations. Generalisation occurs more readily when SST has a clear focus and patients are highly motivated to reach realistic goals, with skills taught being suitable for specific patients.

# Psychodynamic therapies

**psychodynamic therapies** treatment of depression that aims to gain insight into the unconscious mind to reduce psychic tension

**Psychodynamic therapies** have their origins in Freud's psychoanalytic theory and come in varying forms. Psychoanalysis is an intensive form, consisting of several sessions a week for lengthy periods, traditionally conducted with the patient lying on a couch. Psychoanalytic psychotherapy is a less intensive form, consisting of fewer sessions per week and over a shorter period, with therapist and patient in a face-to-face scenario.

The psychodynamic approach traces the roots of depression to childhood, and therefore psychodynamic therapy attempts to explore the patient's past and then link this to their current situation, with childhood experiences of loss and rejection especially seen as crucial depression-forming factors. A patient is encouraged to relive these experiences, which may involve them becoming angry and upset, and these emotions are then discharged in a process known as catharsis (the safe release of negative emotions). The patient therefore gains insight into their inability to form healthy relationships, often a key feature of depression, especially when there is transference on to others of anger caused by early rejection and loss.

## Research

- De Clerq et al. (1999) performed research indicating that psychodynamic therapy, as a treatment for depression, is desirable and feasible when delivered by skilled, well-trained nurses under close supervision. This suggests that the treatment's effectiveness is dependent upon the quality of the clinicians administering it and that therefore the training of therapists is paramount to the therapy's success.
- Burnand et al. (2002) investigated 74 depressed patients between 29 and 65 years of age, to compare treatment by antidepressants alone and treatment by psychotherapy and antidepressants combined. They found marked improvement in both treatment groups, though the combined treatment was associated with less treatment failure, better work adjustment and better global functioning. Because there was a cost saving of $2,311 per patient with the combined treatment, due to lower hospitalisation rates and fewer lost work days, the combined treatment can be seen as superior in terms of cost-effectiveness.
- Carreira et al. (2009) evaluated the effect of psychotherapy on recurrence rates and time to recurrence of major depression in elderly patients over a 2-year period, finding that psychotherapy gave protection against recurrence of the disorder in elderly patients with low cognitive functioning. This suggests that psychotherapy can be targeted effectively at specific groups of patients.
- Leichsenring et al. (2004) reviewed several studies of brief dynamic therapy (BDT), a more modern and simpler form of psychodynamic treatment, finding the therapy to be as effective as cognitive behavioural therapy in addressing depression.

**Knowledge check 24**

What does research suggest about the effectiveness of (a) behavioural therapies and (b) psychodynamic therapies, as treatments for depression?

## Evaluation

- Psychotherapy requires the evaluation of thoughts and behaviour, and those people who become actively involved with their treatment are the ones who recover from depression more quickly and suffer fewer relapses.
- As well as reducing and eradicating specific symptoms, psychotherapy can be very helpful in monitoring and managing suicide risk and ensuring compliance with medical and psychosocial intervention programmes.
- Psychotherapy works best when patients attend all of their scheduled sessions, which requires motivation and effort on the part of the patient, not always easy to achieve with those exhibiting symptoms of depression.
- Eysenck (1952) reviewed several studies of psychotherapy, and found that only 44% of patients improved, compared to 66% of patients who got better through **spontaneous remission** (i.e. without any form of treatment), suggesting psychotherapy to be less effective than not treating patients at all.

# Cognitive behavioural therapy (CBT)

Cognitive behavioural therapy (CBT) has proven to be the main psychological treatment used to combat depression, an indicator in itself of its effectiveness. The main idea behind the therapy is that beliefs, expectations and cognitive assessments of self, the environment and the nature of personal problems affect how a person perceives themselves and others, how problems are approached and how successful a person is in coping and attaining goals. Therefore CBT assists patients in identifying irrational and maladaptive thoughts and altering them. Thoughts are perceived as affecting emotions and thus behaviour too, therefore it is the patient's thinking that has to be altered for reduction of depressive symptoms to occur.

Drawings are often employed to display the links between a sufferer's thoughts, actions and emotions, with comprehension of where symptoms come from being very useful in reducing their anxiety levels. Generally treatment involves one or two sessions of CBT every 2 weeks for an average of about 15 sessions.

**cognitive behavioural therapy (CBT)** treatment of depression that attempts to modify thought patterns to alter behavioural and emotional states

### Research

- Whitfield and Williams (2003) assessed the worth of CBT, finding it to have the strongest research base for effectiveness, but recognised there was a problem in the National Health Service being able to deliver weekly face-to-face sessions for patients. They suggested that such face-to-face contact could be reduced by introducing self-help versions of the treatment, and discussed the SPIRIT course, which teaches clinicians how to offer core cognitive behavioural skills using structured self-help materials.
- The Department of Health (2001) reviewed research papers on treatments for depression, including behavioural, cognitive, humanistic and psychotherapeutic ones, finding CBT to be the most effective compared to other therapies. However, they did not find an overwhelming endorsement for the use of CBT alone, as there was evidence to support the effectiveness of other treatments, such as behavioural therapy. It was also concluded that there was little research that had considered the cost-effectiveness of the various treatments.

**Knowledge check 25**

What does research suggest about the effectiveness of CBT in treating depression?

**Examiner tip**

Always read questions carefully, as they detail the exact requirements. For example, if a question asks for an outline of one psychological therapy and more than one is provided, only the best one is credited. If a question asks for an outline of two therapies and only one is given, then, however detailed and accurate, marks will be limited.

- The National Institute for Mental Health (1994) found CBT to be less effective than antidepressant drugs and other psychological therapies in treating the symptoms of depression, though there is possibly a problem in using assessment methods with CBT which were specifically designed to investigate the worth of biologically-based drug treatments.
- Flannaghan et al. (1997) used a questionnaire to identify stroke victims who had developed clinical depression, and 19 such patients were then given CBT sessions over a 4-month period. A significant decrease in depression occurred during the treatment period, suggesting that CBT may be a suitable treatment for specific groups of depressives.

## Evaluation

- CBT is generally regarded as the most effective psychological treatment for moderate and severe depression and one of the most effective treatments where depression is the main problem.
- For those patients who have difficulty concentrating (a common experience for depressives), CBT can be problematic, leading to a feeling of being overwhelmed and disappointed, which can strengthen depressive symptoms rather than reducing them.
- One problem with CBT, as with all 'talking therapies', is that it might not be suitable for those patients who have difficulties discussing their inner feelings, or for those who do not possess the verbal skills to do so.
- One of the advantages of CBT as a general treatment of depression compared to other forms of treatment is that it produces little in the way of side effects.

**Summary**

- Depression is a mood disorder, occurring in unipolar and bipolar forms, involving prolonged and fundamental disturbance of emotion and is diagnosed by symptoms listed in classification systems.
- Both the reliability and validity of diagnosis are regarded as reasonably high.
- Biological explanations include roles for genetics, evolution and biochemistry.
- Psychological explanations focus on behaviourist learning experiences, as well as psychodynamic, cognitive and sociocultural factors.
- The two main biological treatments of depression are drug therapies involving antidepressants and ECT.
- Psychological treatments for depression include behavioural and psychodynamic therapies and the more favoured cognitive behavioural therapy (CBT).

# Anxiety disorders

## Specification content

- *Clinical characteristics of the chosen disorder*
- *Issues surrounding the classification and diagnosis of the disorder, including reliability and validity*
- *Biological explanations of the disorder, for example genetics, biochemistry*
- *Psychological explanations of the disorder, for example behavioural, cognitive, psychodynamic and sociocultural*
- *Biological therapies for the disorder, including their evaluation in terms of appropriateness and effectiveness*
- *Psychological therapies for the disorder, for example behavioural, psychodynamic and cognitive behavioural, including their evaluation in terms of appropriateness and effectiveness*

There will be two optional questions on anxiety disorders on the examination paper, one on phobic disorders and one on OCD. To ensure that you can answer them, you need to study and understand all of the above.

Clinical characteristics refer to symptoms and types of anxiety disorders that a sufferer may experience and you need a good working knowledge of these. Symptoms are listed within classification systems and you should also have knowledge and understanding of issues of reliability (consistency) and validity (accuracy) associated with classifying and diagnosing anxiety disorders.

Biological and psychological explanations are listed in the specification, so you need to cover both, though the specific explanations given (e.g. psychodynamic) are listed only as examples, meaning that they would not feature explicitly in any examination question. This also means that any other explanations, as long as they are biological or psychological, would be equally acceptable to study.

Finally, the specification focuses on biological and psychological therapies. Again the specific therapies referred to are listed only as examples, meaning that they cannot feature directly in any examination question and that any other therapies, as long as they are biological or psychological, would be equally acceptable to study. There is also a requirement to be able to evaluate both biological and psychological therapies in terms of how appropriate and effective they are.

This part of the guide covers two types of anxiety disorder: phobic disorders and obsessive–compulsive disorder. Note that you only need to study one of these to ensure that you can answer any examination question on anxiety disorders.

## Clinical characteristics of anxiety disorders

Everybody periodically experiences anxiety and this is a normal occurrence — indeed, at times it is healthy to be anxious, for example when in threatening situations or on occasions when we wish to perform well, such as in sporting competitions. However, about one in five people will at some time experience anxiety levels so high that they become maladaptive and negatively affect day-to-day functioning. There are a

**anxiety disorders**
abnormal conditions characterised by extreme worry, fear and nervousness

number of anxiety disorders, all of which have the shared characteristic of fear. This section concentrates on phobic disorders and obsessive–compulsive disorder.

**phobic disorders**
anxiety disorders that are characterised by extreme irrational fears

Phobic disorders are characterised by extreme, irrational and enduring fears that cannot be controlled and involve anxiety levels far out of proportion to any actual risk. It is difficult to estimate accurately the occurrence rate of phobic disorders, as many sufferers attempt to deal with the condition themselves and do not seek clinical aid. What is known is that phobic disorders are about twice as common among females and that around 10% of the population suffer from a specific phobia at some point, with most phobias originating in childhood and diminishing in strength during adulthood.

Agoraphobia, a fear of open spaces, is a common phobia, often occurring with panic disorder, where the sufferer endures the panic disorder first, with the anxiety generated then making the sufferer feel vulnerable about being in open spaces. Social phobias are also quite common and generally involve being over-anxious about activities in social environments, such as talking in public or eating out with people. There are also simple phobias where sufferers have fears of specific things and environments: for example astraphobia, an extreme fear of thunderstorms, or pediophobia, a severe fear of dolls. Animal phobias tend to have the earliest onset, followed by other simple phobias, social phobias and then agoraphobia.

**obsessive–compulsive disorder (OCD)**
an anxiety disorder characterised by persistent, recurrent, unpleasant thoughts and repetitive, ritualistic behaviours

Obsessive–compulsive disorder (OCD) occurs in about 2% of the population, with sufferers enduring persistent and intrusive thoughts that occur as obsessions, compulsions or a combination of both. Obsessions consist of forbidden or inappropriate ideas and visual images that lead to feelings of extreme anxiety, whereas compulsions consist of intense, uncontrollable urges to repetitively perform tasks and behaviours, such as constantly cleaning door handles. Most OCD sufferers have insight into the fact that their compulsions are inappropriate, but cannot exert conscious control over them, resulting in even greater levels of anxiety.

Both phobias and OCD can be seen as exaggerated versions of quite normal behaviour and are perceived as being mental disorders when they become detrimental to normal, everyday functioning — for instance, when the fear of open spaces prevents an agoraphobic from leaving the house to go to a place of work.

## Symptoms of phobic disorders

The symptoms of phobic disorders are as follows:

**Examiner tip**
For questions asking for an outline of clinical characteristics of anxiety disorders, use could be made not only of descriptions of clinical characteristics, but also of symptoms and subtypes, as these also can be considered to contain elements of clinical characteristics.

- **persistent, excessive fear** — a high level of anxiety is caused by the presence or anticipation of a feared object or situation
- **fear from exposure to phobic stimulus** — an immediate fear response, or even a panic attack, is caused by presentation of the phobic object or situation
- **recognition of exaggerated anxiety** — the sufferer is aware that the level of anxiety is excessive
- **avoidant/anxiety response** — feared objects and situations are avoided or lead to high anxiety response
- **disruption of functioning** — the anxiety/avoidance response is so extreme that it severely interferes with the ability to carry out everyday work and social functions

## Subtypes of phobias

Phobias can be divided into simple and social phobias and agoraphobia. Simple phobias can also be further divided into several subtypes:

- **animal phobias** — e.g. arachnophobia (fear of spiders)
- **injury phobias** — e.g. haematophobia (fear of blood)
- **situational phobias** — e.g. aerophobia (fear of flying)
- **natural environment phobias** — e.g. hydrophobia (fear of water)

## Symptoms of OCD

The symptoms of OCD are as follows:

**Obsessions are:**

- **recurrent and persistent** — thoughts, impulses and images are recurrently experienced that are inappropriate and intrusive, leading to high levels of anxiety and distress
- **irrelevant to real life** — thoughts, impulses and images experienced are not relevant to real-life situations
- **suppressed** — the sufferer attempts to suppress thoughts, impulses and images with alternative thoughts or actions
- **recognised as self-generated** — the sufferer recognises that the obsessional thoughts, impulses and images are a product of their own invention and not inserted externally

**Compulsions are:**

- **repetitive** — the sufferer feels compelled to repeat behaviours and mental acts in response to obsessional thoughts, impulses and images
- **aimed at reducing distress** — behaviours and mental acts are an attempt to reduce distress or prevent a feared event, even though they have little realistic chance of doing so

**Other symptoms are:**

- **recognised as excessive** — the sufferer realises that obsessions/compulsions are excessive
- **time-consuming** — obsessions/compulsions are time-consuming, cause distress and interfere with the ability to carry out everyday work and social functions
- **not related to substance abuse** — the disorder is not related to substance abuse or another medical condition

# Issues surrounding the classification and diagnosis of anxiety disorders

This section deals with issues of reliability and validity in relation to the classification and diagnosis of anxiety disorders.

## Reliability

Reliability refers to the **consistency** of measurements and affects the classification and diagnosis of anxiety disorders in two ways:

**Knowledge check 26**
It is normal and healthy to experience anxiety, but when does anxiety develop into phobias?

**Knowledge check 27**
Why is OCD classed as an anxiety disorder?

reliability consistency of diagnosis

- **Test–retest reliability** occurs when a practitioner makes the same consistent diagnosis on separate occasions from the same information.
- **Inter-rater reliability** occurs when several practitioners make identical, independent diagnoses of the same patient.

Even with physical medical disorders, diagnoses are not always reliable, and making reliable diagnoses of anxiety disorders is more problematic, as the practitioner has no physical signs but only symptoms (what the patient reports) on which to base a decision.

### Research: phobic disorders

- Silverman et al. (2001) examined the test–retest reliability of phobic disorders in 62 children between 7 and 16 years of age. The Anxiety Disorders Interview Schedule for DSM-IV was administered twice, with an interval of 7 to 14 days, with results indicating reliability for simple and social phobias.
- Mataix-Cols et al. (2005) studied the reliability of The Work and Social Adjustment Scale (WSAS), a widely used five-item measure of disability, in 205 phobic patients. Internal consistency was found to be very high and the WSAS was concluded to be a reliable measure of work and social adjustment in phobics, though simple phobics had less consistent ratings across WSAS items, suggesting some items were less relevant to their disorder.
- Alström et al. (2009) assessed the inter-rater reliability of phobic disorder diagnosis in Swedish patients, finding it to be very good, with a concordance rate of around 90%.

### Research: OCD

- Geller et al. (2006) assessed the reliability of the Child Behaviour Checklist (CBCL) in the diagnosis of OCD in children, finding it to be reliable and to have acceptable psychometric properties to help discriminate children with OCD.
- Di Nardo and Barlow (1987) found that the principal diagnosis of OCD was associated with excellent diagnostic reliability, scoring an 80% concordance rate, second only to that of simple phobias among anxiety and mood disorders.
- Foa et al. (1987), using Likert scales, obtained strong correlations among patients', therapists' and independent observers' ratings of various OCD features, including main fear, avoidance and compulsion severity, suggesting good inter-rater reliability.

### Knowledge check 28

What has research suggested about the reliability of diagnosis of phobias and OCD?

## Evaluation: phobic disorders

- Silverman and Saavedra (1998) argue that the use of diagnostic interview procedures has greatly enhanced the inter-rater reliability of diagnoses.
- Assessment of inter-rater reliability generally involves one rater interviewing a child and another observing the same interview either live or on video. Therefore both diagnoses are based on the identical information given in the interview, which not surprisingly produces high levels of reliability. A better method would be for one rater to perform an interview and the second rater to perform a separate independent interview of the same patient.
- Research studies differ in the assessment of reliability even when the same measuring scales are used. Early assessments of the Anxiety Disorders Interview Schedule found low levels of reliability for phobic disorders, while later studies found high levels, suggesting it was the revision of measuring scales that led to improved reliability of diagnosis.

## Evaluation: OCD

- Several factors suggest an acute need for a simple, quick, reliable diagnostic tool to identify cases of OCD: its high prevalence in young people, its secretive nature, which leads to under-recognition, and the lack of specialised child psychiatry services in many areas.
- The American Psychiatric Association (1987) reported that, compared to other anxiety disorders, the diagnostic reliability of OCD was quite favourable.
- The fact that OCD has easily observable symptoms assists clear diagnosis of the disorder and thus contributes to high levels of reliability (indeed the same could also be argued for the diagnosis of phobias).

# Validity

Validity concerns how accurate, meaningful and useful diagnosis is. There are a number of ways in which validity can be assessed, for instance:

- **Reliability:** a valid diagnosis has first to be reliable (though reliability itself is no guarantee of validity).
- **Predictive validity:** if diagnosis leads to successful treatment, then the diagnosis can be seen as valid.
- **Descriptive validity:** for diagnosis to be valid, patients diagnosed with different disorders should actually differ from each other. Descriptive validity is reduced by comorbidity, where patients are seen as having two or more disorders simultaneously, suggesting that such disorders are not actually separate from each other.
- **Aetiological validity:** for diagnosis to be valid, all patients diagnosed with anxiety disorders should have the same cause for their disorder.

**validity** accuracy of diagnosis

### Research: phobic disorders

- Herbert et al. (1992) assessed the descriptive validity of social phobias, comparing them with avoidant personality disorder (APD) on a number of variables, including anxiety levels and social skills. They found social phobias and APD to represent quantitatively, but not qualitatively, distinct disorders, suggesting social phobias are not a separate disorder.
- Eysenck (1997) also found descriptive validity to be poor, reporting that around 65% of patients with an anxiety disorder also had other anxiety disorders, again implying subtypes of anxiety disorders not to be independent of each other.
- Vasey and Dadds (2001) tested the predictive validity of anxiety disorder diagnoses, finding few differences in treatment outcomes for the different subgroups, suggesting low predictive validity.

### Research: OCD

- Leckman and Chittenden (1990), assessing the validity of diagnosis of OCD, found that up to 50% of patients with Tourette's syndrome also had OCD, suggesting OCD not to be a separate disorder.
- Scahill et al. (1997) assessed the validity of the Children's Yale-Brown Obsessive Compulsive Scale (CY-BOCS), applying it to 65 children and adolescents with OCD. They found that validity was influenced by age and the difficulties involved with integrating data from parental and patient sources.
- Deacon and Abramovitz (2004) tested the validity of the Yale-Brown Obsessive Compulsive Scale (Y-BOCS), regarded as the gold-standard measure of OCD, by applying it to 100 patients with a diagnosis of OCD. They found that there were problems with the Y-BOCS sub-scales' ability to validly measure the components of OCD, suggesting the scales need serious revision.

**Knowledge check 29**

What has research indicated about the validity of diagnosis of phobias and OCD?

## Evaluation: phobic disorders

- The predictive validity of diagnostic systems relating to children's anxiety disorders has been subject to little research. Those studies done indicate little evidence of childhood anxiety disorders predicting different outcomes, suggesting low predictive validity.
- Validation of diagnostic scales is important not only in proving such criteria as valid in themselves, but because such diagnostic scales can then be used to further assess the validity of other diagnostic measures.
- Rabung et al. (2009) believe that self-rating instruments can be valid measuring tools of phobic anxiety, as they are sensitive to change, suitable for clinical use and cost-effective (because they can be downloaded free from the internet).

## Evaluation: OCD

- Diagnoses of OCD can have a long-term negative impact on sufferers' lives and yet such diagnoses may be being made with little evidence of the disorder existing as a separate condition.
- Although evidence indicates that many measuring scales used to assess OCD are not valid, they are still regarded as the most effective assessment tool in determining diagnostic and treatment outcomes.
- Thordarson et al. (2003) report that the revision of measuring scales for OCD can lead to more valid diagnoses, which is important as this will promote a better understanding of the disorder.

# Biological explanations of anxiety disorders

Biological explanations have focused on several areas, including genetics, evolution and biochemical influences. Evidence relating to genetic factors has tended to focus on gene mapping and on twin and family studies. Overall, evidence indicates a contributory role for biological factors, although environmental factors also seem to be involved in the onset of anxiety disorders.

## Genetic explanations

Research has traditionally used twin and family studies to assess what role, if any, genetic explanations might play in the causation of anxiety disorders. Results from these sources indicate some genetic influence, though one of the problems with such studies is separating out environmental influences.

More recently, technology has advanced, allowing gene mapping studies to be undertaken. This entails comparing genetic material from families with a high and low incidence of anxiety disorders. Results from gene mapping indicate that particular genes are involved and that these genes make some individuals more vulnerable than others to developing the disorder. Therefore genes probably do not cause anxiety disorders on their own: indeed, if they did, the concordance rate between MZ (monozygotic or identical) twins would be 100%, which it clearly is not.

### Research: phobic disorders

- Kendler et al. (1992) examined 2,163 female twin pairs, finding a 24.4% concordance rate for social phobia in MZ (identical) twins, compared to only 15.3% for DZ (dizygotic or non-identical) twins, suggesting a genetic influence.
- Reich and Yates (1988) interviewed social phobics from an anxiety treatment clinic and used information on first-degree relatives to assess the inheritance of the disorder. They found the rate of social phobia to be higher in relatives of social phobics (6.6%) than in relatives of non-social phobic controls (2.2%), suggesting some genetic influence.
- Gelertner et al. (2004) conducted a gene mapping study on sufferers of social phobias, and found a link to social phobias for various markers of chromosome 16, with additional interest also centred on chromosomes 9, 14 and 18, suggesting a genetic component to the disorder.

**Examiner tip**
Students often confuse the relationship between reliability and validity. A valid diagnosis must be reliable (consistent), but a reliable diagnosis doesn't guarantee validity (accuracy). For example adding up 1 + 1 several times and always getting the answer 3 is reliable but isn't valid. Adding up 1 + 1 several times and always getting 2 is however both reliable and valid.

**biological explanations** anxiety disorders perceived as having a physiological cause

**genetic explanations** anxiety disorders perceived as transmitted by hereditary means

## Evaluation: phobic disorders

- Although research indicates some genetic involvement in the onset of phobic disorders, the evidence is stronger for other mental disorders, such as schizophrenia.
- A case can be made for explaining the onset of phobic disorders in terms of the **diathesis–stress model**, where individuals inherit different degrees of vulnerability, but it is environmental triggers that ultimately determine whether an individual actually goes on to develop the disorder.
- Although evidence from twin and family studies suggests a genetic influence, it may be that related individuals acquire phobias through similar environmental experiences, or through imitation.

**Research: OCD**

- Lenane et al. (1990) undertook a study into the prevalence of OCD among related family members, and found evidence for the existence of heritable contributions to the onset of the disorder, lending support to the genetic viewpoint.
- Grootheest et al. (2005) reviewed 70 years of twin studies into OCD, and found a heritability rate of between 45% and 65% for OCD in children and between 27% and 47% in adults, again suggesting a genetic contribution.
- Samuels et al. (2007) used gene mapping to compare OCD sufferers who exhibit compulsive hoarding behaviour with those who do not, and found a link to chromosome 14 marker D14S588, suggesting a genetic influence on compulsive hoarding behaviour, which may also indicate the existence of separate OCD subtypes.

## Evaluation: OCD

- Weissman (1985) noted that the tendency for anxiety disorders, such as OCD, to run in families was first observed over a century ago; therefore such an idea is not new and has greatly influenced subsequent research.
- Evidence from family and twin studies indicates genetic factors at work in the expression of some forms of OCD, especially obsessions about contamination, aggression and religion, and compulsions involving washing, ordering and arranging.
- The fact that family members often display dissimilar OCD symptoms, for example a child arranging dolls and an adult constantly washing dishes, weakens support for the genetic viewpoint, because if the disorder was inherited then exhibited behaviours would be the same.

## Evolutionary explanations

Anxiety disorders continue to be apparent in the population and historical evidence indicates they have existed for a very long time. These facts suggest

**Examiner tip**

When revising material for the psychopathology section of your Unit 4 examination, ensure that you have prepared material for both a short and a longer version of answers requiring an outline. Sometimes an outline may be worth just 4 marks, but at other times 8 marks. A different amount of material would therefore be required for these questions.

evolutionary explanations, in that they have an adaptive value linked to survival. If the disorder served no useful purpose, then the evolutionary viewpoint would argue that the process of natural selection would have selected it out and the condition would no longer exist. This view of the origins of anxiety disorders differs in seeing the disorders not as maladaptive but as fulfilling a beneficial purpose.

Seligman (1971) introduced the idea of **biological preparedness**, where animals have an innate ability to display certain fears, because they serve an adaptive function linked to survival and reproduction. Therefore animals develop some conditioned fears more easily, for instance a dread of spiders, as they would have constituted a serious threat in the evolutionary past (the 'environment of evolutionary adaptedness' or EEA). Such fears have both a genetic and an environmental component, as the phobia has to be learned from environmental experience, with the predisposition to learn the fear being the inherited component.

Phobias can serve several adaptive functions. For instance, the fear element of a phobia can result in cessation of movement, freezing an individual on the spot, which may aid concealment from predators; similarly, a flight response would help a person to outrun such predators. Alternatively, fear could bend an individual into submission to dominant aggressors, saving them from harm. The fear response may even cause the release of hormones that aid the clotting of blood to help heal wounds, as well as stimulating the liver to release glucose to provide energy, important to facilitate fight or flight.

OCD often involves such repetitive behaviours as washing and grooming, which would have been important in the EEA in preventing infection; other similar behaviours may have been linked to increased vigilance and alertness, which again would have had a survival value. Modern-day versions of these behaviours, such as continually cleaning door handles, can be seen as exaggerations of ancient adaptations.

## Research: phobic disorders

- Garcia and Koelling (1966) found that rats quickly learned not to drink a sweet-tasting liquid paired with an injection that made them sick, as it is a natural adaptive response, but did not develop such a taste aversion when the sweet-tasting liquid was paired with an electric shock, as it is not an adaptive response (since electric shocks would not have been experienced in the EEA). This supports the idea of biological preparedness.
- Cook and Mineka (1989) demonstrated to laboratory-raised monkeys the fear response of a wild monkey to a snake and a rabbit. Subsequently the laboratory-raised monkeys showed a similar fear response to a toy snake, but not to a toy rabbit, suggesting an evolutionary readiness to fear snakes, but not rabbits.
- Bennett-Levy and Marteau (1984) got participants to rate 29 animals for ugliness, fearsomeness and harmfulness. The less human an animal appeared, the bigger the fear response, again suggesting an adaptive readiness to fear certain things more than others.

evolutionary explanations anxiety disorders perceived as having an adaptive value linked to survival

**Examiner tip**

When describing biological explanations of anxiety disorders, such as the evolutionary explanation, it may be necessary to outline the explanation in general, for example that evolutionary explanations see an adaptive advantage to human qualities and behaviours. However, answers that are not specifically oriented at explaining how evolutionary theory views anxiety disorders will earn little, if any, credit.

**Knowledge check 30**

How do the following biological explanations perceive the causes of phobias and OCD: (a) the genetic explanation; (b) the evolutionary explanation?

**Research: OCD**

- Abed and Pauw (1998) believe OCD to be an exaggerated form of an evolved ability to foresee future situations and predict the outcome of one's own thoughts and behaviour, so that dangerous scenarios can be coped with before they even occur, suggesting that OCD helps in the avoidance of harm.
- Marks and Nesse (1984) state that a lack of concern for others incurs a risk of ostracism from the social group, so the fact that many OCD sufferers have a great concern for the welfare of others suggests it has an adaptive value in reducing this risk.
- Chepko-Sade et al. (1989) found that rhesus monkeys who performed the most grooming of others were retained within a group following group in-fighting, suggesting that such OCD tendencies have an adaptive value, as continued group membership is crucial to survival.

## Evaluation: phobic disorders

- The concept of biological preparedness explains why it is harder to develop fears of dangerous modern-day objects and situations, such as guns, because they did not exist in the EEA and thus a readiness to fear them is not coded into our genes.
- Some phobias are so bizarre and individual that they are better explained as being purely conditioned responses, rather than having an evolved component.
- Evolutionary explanations of phobias can be regarded as deterministic, as they tend not to account for individual and cultural differences.

## Evaluation: OCD

- Behavioural features of OCD, such as counting and hoarding, can be seen as beneficial in the hunting and gathering of food and therefore would have been useful in the EEA. It could be argued that they remain now due to **genome lag**, whereby genes take time to evolve and better fit the current environment.
- It is possible to perceive OCD as produced by the process of evolution and thus having a genetic basis, leading to neuroanatomical and biochemical influences.

## Biochemical explanations

biochemical explanations anxiety disorders perceived as determined by the actions of neurotransmitters and hormones

Evidence does not tend to suggest that biochemical explanations can provide a sole explanation of anxiety disorders. However, it is thought that biochemical factors do play an important part in determining an individual's level of vulnerability.

Research has centred on the amino acid GABA, which is indicated to be involved in the control of arousal and anxiety levels. GABA lowers anxiety levels by suppressing nervous system activity. Certain individuals, however, appear to be more susceptible to environmental influences and thus have above-average levels of physical arousal and anxiety, and this is seen as being related to abnormal GABA functioning.

**Neurotransmitters** are chemicals found within the body, which act upon its biology and are associated with the transmission of signals through the nervous system, especially with sending signals across the gaps between nerve fibres during the process known as synapse. Abnormal neurotransmitter activity has been associated with OCD, and research attention has been directed at reduced levels of serotonin and elevated levels of dopamine in sufferers. SSRIs are drugs commonly used to combat depression, but they also have the beneficial effect of reducing symptoms of OCD by stopping serotonin being broken down and thus elevating its level in the brain. Conversely, drugs that reduce serotonin levels increase symptoms. SSRIs have also been seen to reduce the symptoms of phobias and so serotonin may also be involved there.

### Research: phobic disorders

- Sahley (2001) reports that social phobics have an altered brain structure characterised by low serotonin levels and an overactive limbic system. When neurotransmitter deficiencies are treated with amino acids such as GABA, symptoms are reduced, supporting the idea of such phobias being related to a dysfunctional GABA system.
- Benjamin et al. (2000) gave patients suffering from specific phobias serotonin-enhancing drugs and found symptoms were significantly reduced, which suggests a link between specific phobias and reduced serotonin functioning.
- Van Vliet et al. (1993) treated 30 social phobic patients with the SSRI fluvoxamine for 12 weeks and found that 47% of patients showed improvements in their condition compared to only 7% of patients given a placebo, suggesting that serotonin levels might be implicated in social anxiety.

### Research: OCD

- Fineberg (1996) found that the symptoms of OCD were reduced in patients taking SSRIs, which increase levels of serotonin in the brain, while Hollander et al. (1988) found symptoms worsen with serotonin agonists, which reduce serotonin levels. These findings support the serotonin hypothesis.
- Van Ameringen et al. (2001) performed research on transgenically engineered mice that suggested general OCD is linked to abnormal serotonin functioning, while tic-related OCD, such as Tourette's syndrome, is more associated with abnormal dopamine functioning, suggesting that OCD might not really be an anxiety disorder at all.
- Insel et al. (1991) reported that three drugs, clomipramine, Prozac and fluvoxamine, all of which stimulate serotonin production in the nervous system, benefit OCD patients, with about 50% showing improvements, supporting the serotonin hypothesis.

## Evaluation: phobic disorders

- The successful treatment of phobias with GABA and SSRIs provides strong evidence of a role for biochemistry in the development of phobias.
- Drugs may address the physical symptoms associated with phobias, but not the actual disorder itself. When drug treatment stops, phobic symptoms tend to return.
- Evidence suggests that phobias do not occur due to low serotonin functioning, but rather that low serotonin functioning makes a person more susceptible to becoming phobic due to environmental experiences.

### Examiner tip

An excellent way of producing high-quality answers to questions on explanation of anxiety orders is to illustrate how factors can be combined. For example, with biochemical explanations, the neurotransmitter serotonin can be a sole explanation of phobias but also relates to a dysfunctional GABA system to offer a more sophisticated explanation of how they collectively influence anxiety disorders.

### Knowledge check 31

How do biochemical explanations perceive the causes of phobias and OCD?

### Evaluation: OCD

- Psychological treatments for OCD have proven successful but do not elevate serotonin levels, weakening support for the serotonin hypothesis.
- The ability of serotonin-enhancing drugs to alleviate the symptoms of OCD is reduced because their side effects cause many patients to stop taking them.
- Even where evidence links biochemistry to the experience of OCD, it is not clear whether biochemical factors are a cause or merely an effect of the disorder.

# Psychological explanations of anxiety disorders

psychological explanations anxiety disorders perceived as having non-physiological causes

Although evidence indicates that biological factors play an important role in the onset of anxiety disorders, it is generally accepted that psychological factors are involved too. There are several psychological explanations of anxiety disorders, including the behaviourist, psychodynamic, cognitive and sociocultural explanations.

## Behaviourist explanations

behaviourist explanations anxiety disorders perceived as determined through learning processes

Classical conditioning explains phobias as occurring through the association of traumatic events with neutral stimuli, with the resulting phobias then becoming resistant to extinction, because of the avoidance responses made to feared objects or situations. Operant conditioning can then explain how phobias are maintained, as when avoidance responses are made the fear element is reduced, which reinforces the avoidance responses, making them more likely to occur again. For example, if an individual has a phobia of the dark, due to a traumatic event occurring at night-time, then the phobic is likely to sleep with the lights on, which reduces the fear element and increases the chances the sufferer will make the same avoidance response again and sleep with the lights on.

Operant conditioning can also be used to explain the maintenance of OCD: if a sufferer experiences anxiety, for instance about dirt and infection, then thoroughly washing all the door handles is reinforcing, as it reduces the anxiety and makes the behaviour likely to recur. Skinner's (1948) **superstition hypothesis** can also be used to explain OCD, where bodily actions become associated with a reinforcer and thus are repeated. For example, not stepping on the cracks in the pavement becomes associated with a reduction in anxiety.

**Social learning theory** can also explain phobias as occurring through observation and imitation of others, as merely watching another person experience a traumatic event can cause the observer to subsequently experience the fear response in the presence of the same stimulus.

- Watson and Rayner (1920) conditioned 'Little Albert' to fear white furry objects by pairing the neutral stimulus of a white rat with the unconditioned stimulus of a sudden loud noise to produce an innate fear response, demonstrating how phobias can be learned by classical conditioning.
- Gray (1975) used the **two-process theory** to explain how operant conditioning can strengthen phobias acquired through classical conditioning. A phobia is first learned by a specific event being paired with the fear response and then an avoidance response is learned that reduces the fear element, thus strengthening the avoidance response.
- Ost and Hugdahl (1981) reported on the case of a boy who witnessed his grandfather vomit while dying and subsequently developed a strong and persistent vomiting phobia; indeed, he even later contemplated suicide when feeling nauseous, supporting the idea that phobias can be acquired vicariously through social learning experiences.

**Research: OCD**

- Meyer and Cheeser (1970) demonstrated how compulsions are learned responses that can reduce the heightened anxiety levels brought on by obsessions, thus providing a behaviourist explanation for elements of the disorder.
- Einstein and Menzies (2003) gave 60 OCD patients the Magical Ideation Scale, which measures beliefs in magical thinking, and found a significant correlation between magical thinking and OCD symptoms, suggesting a link between superstition and OCD in line with Skinner's superstition hypothesis.
- Carr (1974) reported that ritualised behaviours were demonstrated when activity in a sufferer's autonomic nervous system (ANS) was heightened and such behaviour then led to a reduction of arousal in the ANS, suggesting that compulsive behaviours are reinforcing as they reduce the anxiety levels associated with OCD.

## Evaluation: phobic disorders

- The success of behaviourist treatments, such as systematic desensitisation, in addressing phobic symptoms lends support to behaviourist explanations of such disorders.
- The behaviourist viewpoint is weakened by the fact that not everyone who experiences a traumatic event, such as a car accident, goes on to develop a phobia.
- One strength of behaviourist explanations is that they can be combined with biological ones to give a better understanding of how phobias occur. An example is the idea of **genetic vulnerability**, whereby some individuals are more susceptible to developing phobias through environmental experiences.

**Examiner tip**

With 24-mark questions requiring an outline and an evaluation (e.g. 'Outline and evaluate explanations of phobias or OCD'), students can overdo the outline, leaving little time for evaluation. The outline is worth only 8 marks while the evaluation is worth 16 marks, so only one-third of the time should be spent on the outline and two-thirds on the evaluation.

### Evaluation: OCD

- Schwartz et al. (1996) reported that behavioural therapies are very effective in reducing the symptoms of OCD and also bring about changes in biochemical activity, lending support to the behaviourist explanation.
- The avoidance behaviours that often characterise OCD and are performed to reduce anxiety, such as persistent washing, can be argued to actually create more anxiety. Therefore it is difficult to view such behaviours as reinforced responses, weakening the behaviourist viewpoint.
- Although certain aspects of OCD can be explained by behaviourism, intrusive thoughts (often a key feature of the disorder) cannot, again weakening such an explanation.

## Psychodynamic explanations

**psychodynamic explanations** anxiety disorders seen as caused by unresolved, repressed childhood traumas

Psychodynamic explanations of phobias see them as **ego defence mechanisms** that help to cope with repressed anxieties. These anxieties become displaced on to a phobic object that symbolises the initial conflict. Once the conflict is dealt with, then the phobia will depart. Bowlby (1973) thought early attachment experiences could also be involved with the onset of phobias, due to a child experiencing separation anxiety or having over-protective parents.

OCD is regarded by the psychodynamic approach as originating through fixations in the anal stage. A child may accept the desire of parents to be neat and tidy, though their natural tendency is to be messy. If the tendency is strong and parents too strict, the child becomes anally fixated. This is seen as occurring at the unconscious level, with the sufferer believing that they really do desire to be neat and tidy. Therefore OCD is perceived as occurring in those who demonstrate anal personality characteristics, such as being very tidy, organised and punctual, and so OCD is viewed as being an exaggeration of the anal personality type. The psychodynamic explanation also regards obsessions as **defence mechanisms** that occupy the mind in order to displace more threatening thoughts.

OCD can also be explained as occurring when the id produces unacceptable urges that create anxiety within the ego and thus are dealt with by ego defence mechanisms such as:

- **isolation** — the ego separates itself from any unacceptable urges, but these can still have an effect as obsessional thoughts
- **undoing** — the ego copes with anxiety by developing compulsive behaviours that symbolically deconstruct (undo) the unacceptable urges
- **reaction formation** — anxiety is reduced by enacting behaviours that are the opposite of the unacceptable urges

Research: phobic disorders

- Knijnik et al. (2004) gave psychodynamic group therapy (PGT) for 12 weeks to patients with social phobias and found their condition improved, lending support to the psychodynamic explanation.
- Salzman (1980) found psychodynamic therapies are generally of little help to clients with specific anxiety disorders, such as phobias and OCD, but may be of help to those with general anxiety disorders, which implies the psychodynamic approach cannot explain phobias or OCD.
- Gerslman et al. (1990) reviewed the available research literature and found that social phobics and agoraphobics had reduced levels of parental affection and heightened levels of over-protective and controlling parents, supporting the psychodynamic approach.

Research: OCD

- Petersen (1992) reported that there is no support for the idea that people who have an obsessive personality style are any more likely to develop OCD than those who do not, weakening support for the psychodynamic approach.
- Fisher and Greenberg (1996) reviewed studies of anal and oral personalities and found no evidence that these types related in any manner to early childhood experiences or 'fixations', again weakening support for the approach.
- Noonan (1971) found that psychoanalysis increases the symptoms of OCD because of the tendency of clients to be over-concerned with their actions and anxious about their condition, severely weakening the psychodynamic argument.

**Knowledge check 32**

How do the following psychological explanations perceive the causes of phobias and OCD:
(a) behaviourist explanations;
(b) psychodynamic explanations?

## Evaluation: phobic disorders

- The psychodynamic approach is based on case studies (in-depth studies of individuals), so the results gained with one person may not be generalisable to others. For instance, several people may have a phobic reaction to an identical stimulus, but for different reasons, reducing the usefulness of the psychodynamic explanation.
- Freud presented the case study of a child, 'Little Hans', as an explanation of phobias, where Hans had a fear of horses that Freud believed was an unconscious fear of his father, the horse's bridle being a representation of his father's moustache. However, Hans's phobia of horses could more easily be explained as due to classical conditioning.
- The psychodynamic approach focuses more upon symbolic meanings of phobic objects, rather than having any empirically based evidence to support it.

**Examiner tip**

Although not an essential requirement for Unit 4 answers, relevant points concerning issues, debates and approaches (IDA) can help form excellent evaluative points. For example, when evaluating the psychodynamic explanation of phobias or OCD, reference could be made to the non-falsifiable nature of the psychodynamic approach.

**cognitive explanations** anxiety disorders perceived as determined through maladaptive thought processes

## Evaluation: OCD

- A big problem with the psychodynamic approach is that it is very difficult to scientifically test the key idea of unconscious motivation, and it therefore becomes very hard to refute or provide support for the model.
- Adler (1931) presented an alternative psychodynamic explanation: OCD arises through a person experiencing feelings of insecurity, inferiority and incompetence.
- The psychodynamic approach sees the roots of OCD as going back to childhood; however, Freud only presented one case study of a child, 'Little Hans', and this study was actually carried out by the boy's father, which goes against the explanation.

# Cognitive explanations

Cognitive explanations see phobias as originating from maladaptive thinking. For example, an overfull bath may generate a belief that open taps are associated with flooding, which turns into a fear of open taps that can even generalise to other scenarios of running water. Therefore the maladaptive thinking is a reaction to an anxiety-generating situation, which then becomes a phobia.

The cognitive viewpoint of OCD, on the other hand, is that sufferers have impaired, persistent thought processes, for example believing that the risk of infection in a given environment is much higher than is actually the case. This type of thinking leads to self-blame, depression and heightened anxiety. Behaviours that decrease the impaired, obsessive thoughts become compulsive because of their anxiety-reducing qualities and thus become difficult to control.

Another cognitive factor concerns the tendency of people with anxiety disorders to be affected by **attentional bias**. For example, phobics concentrate their attention more on anxiety-generating stimuli than other people.

**Research: phobic disorders**

- Thorpe and Salkovskis (2000) assessed conscious beliefs related to exposure to phobic stimuli, and found a major role in specific phobics for cognitions (thinking) related to harm, suggesting the nature of specific phobias to be cognitive in origin.
- Tomarken et al. (1989) investigated the role that distorted thinking plays in phobias. People with snake phobias were presented with slides of neutral objects such as trees as well as slides of snakes, and then asked how many snakes, trees and so on there had been. Those with snake phobias tended to overestimate the number of snakes compared to a control group, lending support to the cognitive explanation.
- Kindt and Brosschot (1997) found that arachnophobics took longer to name the ink colour of spider-related words when performing a Stroop test, which supports the cognitive theory.

**Research: OCD**

- Rachman and Hodges (1987) reported that some individuals are more susceptible to obsessional thinking because of increased vulnerability due to genetic factors, depression or poor socialisation experiences, which links cognitive factors with other explanations.
- Davison and Neale (1994) found that OCD patients cannot distinguish between thoughts and reality, lending support to the idea of a link between faulty thinking processes and OCD.
- Clark (1992) reported that intrusive thinking is significantly more common in OCD sufferers than in the normal population, again supporting the cognitive argument.

## Evaluation: phobic disorders

- One problem with the cognitive viewpoint is that it is not clear whether distorted and negative thinking cause a phobia, or are merely the effect of the phobia.
- The cognitive explanation is deterministic in that it perceives phobias as caused by psychological factors over which the sufferer has no control.
- The cognitive viewpoint can explain how a phobia is maintained, but not why it occurred in the first place. For example, a phobia could be caused by conditioning or genetics and then be perpetuated by faulty thinking.

## Evaluation: OCD

- As with phobias, it is not clear if maladaptive thinking is a cause or an effect of OCD.
- Cognitive treatments of OCD have proven effective by correcting cognitive bias and helping sufferers to become less vigilant, implying support for the cognitive model.
- The cognitive viewpoint does not really explain the emotional aspect of irrational beliefs, weakening support for it.

# Sociocultural explanations

Sociocultural explanations see social and cultural factors as influencing anxiety disorders. For instance, the prevalence of certain phobic disorders seems higher in some cultures than in others and there is evidence that some phobias are culture-specific (i.e. are present only in certain cultures).

OCD seems to occur in a remarkably similar fashion across cultures, suggesting that cultural factors do not play a large role; backing up this impression is the fact that prevalence rates of OCD are also very similar across cultures. However, culture can have an effect on the actual symptoms displayed, which tend to reflect the characteristics of a given culture.

Social factors generally concern the role that family dynamics can play in developing anxiety disorders. For instance, fearful and socially anxious parents could unknowingly transfer information to their children about the dangers of social

**Examiner tip**
A useful way to evaluate both explanations and therapies is to compare different ones, drawing out their appropriateness and effectiveness by contrasting their relative strengths and weaknesses. Questions may even ask for such a comparison, such as 'Critically compare biological and psychological explanations of phobias or OCD.'

**sociocultural explanations** anxiety disorders perceived as being determined through family and social environments

situations and cause the children to develop the same anxiety themselves. In the USA children have been found more likely to develop social phobias if their parents use shame as a form of discipline and place emphasis on the importance of society's opinions.

### Research: phobic disorders

- Kleinknecht et al. (1997) reported on a Japanese form of social phobia known as **taijin kyofusho** (TKS), where sufferers have a fear of offending others with inappropriate behaviour or offensive appearance, suggesting some phobias can be culturally determined.
- Bruch and Heimberg (1994) found that children of parents who were socially isolated tended to be more socially isolated themselves and therefore more at risk of developing social phobias.
- Fritscher (2008) reports that the lifetime prevalence of specific phobias is 8.8% in the USA, but only 0.2% in Northern Ireland, while the 1-year prevalence of social phobias is 45.6% in Udmurtia, but only 0.53% in Korea, suggesting that cultural factors play a strong role in developing phobias worldwide.

### Research: OCD

- Reza Mohammadi et al. (2004) found the rate of OCD in Iran was 1.8%, in line with the consistent rate of the disorder internationally of between 1.9% and 2.5%, suggesting culture has little influence on the prevalence of the disorder.
- Fontenelle et al. (2004) found that obsessions centred on aggression and religious observations were common in Brazilian and Middle Eastern populations, implying that OCD symptoms can take on the characteristics of a given culture.
- Jaisoorya et al. (2008) examined sex differences among 231 OCD sufferers in India, and found that males had an earlier onset of the disorder and more religious obsessions, while females had more cleaning and hair-pulling compulsions, suggesting social factors may be involved.

### Knowledge check 33

How do the following psychological explanations perceive the causes of phobias and OCD:
(a) cognitive explanations;
(b) sociocultural explanations?

## Evaluation: phobic disorders

- The fact that children of parents with an anxiety disorder are more at risk of developing the disorder themselves could as easily be explained in genetic terms as in terms of social factors.
- Media emphasis on demonstrating 'normal' and 'attractive' personal characteristics may also contribute to individuals feeling inferior and insecure and developing social phobias.
- Demographic variables may also be important: for instance, there are lower rates of social phobias in Mediterranean countries and higher ones in Scandinavian countries, maybe because hot weather and high population density increase interpersonal contact.

## Evaluation: OCD

- The fact that prevalence rates of OCD are similar cross-culturally suggests biological factors may be involved.
- One difficulty in assessing prevalence rates of OCD across cultures is that different countries tend to use different criteria to diagnose the disorder, making comparisons difficult.
- The prevalence rate of OCD is very similar for males and females, about 2.5%, again suggesting biological rather than sociocultural factors to be at play.

# Biological therapies for anxiety disorders

This section discusses drug treatments and psychosurgery as biological therapies used for anxiety disorders.

## Drug therapies

Although phobias tend to be treated by psychological means, drug therapies that reduce symptoms of anxiety have proven useful. Anxiolytics are one group of drugs that can achieve this, for example the benzodiazepines (BZs) such as Valium and Librium, which work by increasing the effect of the neurotransmitter GABA. BZs can have side effects, however, such as drowsiness and addiction.

Phobias can also be treated with antidepressants. Selective serotonin reuptake inhibitors (SSRIs) have a beneficial effect by elevating serotonin levels, while monoamine oxidase inhibitors (MAOIs) increase serotonin and noradrenaline levels.

Antidepressants such as SSRIs are also used to treat OCD, and, just as with phobias, anxiolytic drugs can be prescribed too, due to their anxiety-lowering properties. Antipsychotic drugs that have a dopamine-lowering effect have also proven useful in treating the disorder.

Beta-blockers have also had some success in reducing the physical symptoms of anxiety disorders. They work by countering the rise in blood pressure and heart rate often associated with anxiety, by lowering adrenaline and noradrenaline production.

### Research: phobic disorders

- Slaap et al. (1996) treated 30 social phobics with the antidepressant SSRIs brofaromine and fluvoxamine, and found that 72% of patients had reductions in heart rate and blood pressure, suggesting drug treatments to be effective in decreasing the physical symptoms of the disorder.
- Tyrer and Sternberg (1975) followed up for 1 year 26 agoraphobic and social phobic patients who had been treated with the BZ drug phenelzine, and during this time the patients received either further drug treatment or behaviour therapy. It was found that drug treatment was effective, but that it acted mainly by suppressing symptoms, indicating some support for the use of drugs.
- Den Boer et al. (1994) reported that there is considerable evidence that MAOIs, such as moclobemide, are effective in reducing social anxiety and social avoidance, though there is an increased risk of hypertension with their usage.

**biological therapies** treatments of anxiety disorders that are based upon physical methods of intervention

**drug therapies** chemical treatment of abnormality through tablets and intravenous means

**Examiner tip**
Research that finds therapies effective can be used to positively evaluate such therapies, but can additionally be used to support the explanations upon which they are based. Therefore, research detailing the success of drug therapies also backs up the biological approach. However, the treatment aetiology fallacy states that the fact that drugs alleviate symptoms does not necessarily mean they are treating the cause.

- Piccinelli et al. (1995) performed a meta-analysis of 36 studies assessing the worth of antidepressants as a treatment for OCD. They found them to be effective in the short-term treatment of the disorder, with 61% showing improved symptoms with the tricyclic antidepressant clomipramine and 28% with the newer SSRI medications, both treatments proving more beneficial than non-serotonergic drugs.
- Beroqvist et al. (1999) investigated the effect of low doses of the antipsychotic drug risperidone in treating OCD, finding treatment to be effective due to the drug's dopamine-lowering effect.
- Flament et al. (1985) tested the ability of the antidepressant drug clomipramine to address the symptoms of childhood OCD in 19 patients, finding the drug to be superior over a 5-week period to placebo treatment, so lending support to the use of drug treatments.

**Knowledge check 34**

What does research suggest about the effectiveness of drug therapies as a treatment for phobias and OCD?

## Evaluation: phobic disorders

- Aside from their addictive qualities, another problem with BZs is that once patients stop taking them, they can experience a sharp rise in anxiety levels.
- Drug treatments have proven effective in reducing the physical symptoms of phobias so that psychological treatments can then be effectively applied.
- There are those within the psychiatric community who see the widespread use of drug treatments as being fuelled by the powerful influence of the drug-producing companies who stand to make huge profits from their application.

## Evaluation: OCD

- Drug treatments cannot be regarded as a cure for OCD, as symptoms tend to reappear once drug-taking stops.
- Drug treatments are widely used to treat the symptoms of OCD as they are a cost-effective and user-friendly form of treatment.
- It can be argued that drug treatments should not be used for OCD, because of the risk of side effects and the tendency of antidepressants to produce heightened levels of suicidal thinking, and the effectiveness of psychological treatments.

## Psychosurgery

psychosurgery
treatment of anxiety disorders by irreversible destruction of brain tissue

Psychosurgery is occasionally used for severe cases of anxiety disorders that do not respond to other forms of treatment. In this sense psychosurgery can be seen as a last resort, which is reluctantly used, as it entails the usual risks associated with invasive surgery and involves irreversible destruction of tissue, with no guarantee of success. It can also cause serious side effects, such as apathy and reduced intellect. However, there have been recent attempts to use deep brain stimulation, which is reversible, to treat severe cases of OCD.

There are certain criteria that must be met before psychosurgery will be considered:
**(1)** A clinical diagnosis of an anxiety disorder has been made.
**(2)** There are severe symptoms that obstruct purposeful everyday living.
**(3)** Other treatments have failed.
**(4)** The patient has given fully informed consent, with full knowledge of the procedure and the risks involved.

### Research: phobic disorders

- Marks et al. (1966) compared 22 severe agoraphobics who had modified frontal leucotomies with matched cases who had other forms of treatment. They found, 5 years after treatment, that the leucotomies were superior in lessening symptoms to other treatments and that personality changes were only mild, supporting the use of psychosurgery for such patients.
- Ruck et al. (2003) reported that patients who had capsulotomies performed for anxiety disorders, including severe social phobias, generally had large reductions in anxiety levels, demonstrating the technique to be effective, though some patients suffered severe side effects.
- Balon (2003) reported that thermocapsulotomy can be an effective treatment for selected cases of acute non-obsessive anxiety disorders, including phobias, but is an extreme option, as it carries a significant risk of severe side effects.

### Research: OCD

- Kelly and Cobb (1985) reported that 78% of 49 patients suffering from OCD displayed improved symptoms 20 months after limbic leucotomies were performed, suggesting a good level of support for the treatment.
- Hindus et al. (1985) followed up gamma capsulotomy surgical cases 3 and 7 years after treatment, and found that only a few OCD patients showed improvements in their condition, suggesting that different forms of psychosurgery have vastly different success rates.
- Richter et al. (2004) reported that 30% of OCD patients treated with psychosurgery had a 35% or greater reduction in symptoms on the Yale-Brown Obsessive Compulsive Scale. However, there were infrequent complications, such as urinary incontinence and seizures, demonstrating that although psychosurgery can be effective, it is not without its dangers.

### Knowledge check 35

What does research suggest about the effectiveness of psychosurgery as a treatment for phobias and OCD?

## Evaluation: phobic disorders

- Psychosurgery was a more common treatment before the advent of effective behavioural therapies and, for most cases, would not be prescribed nowadays, unless other treatments had not proven useful.
- It seems very improbable that different mental symptoms can be relieved by one single form of operation on the brain; therefore, only operations suitable for precise psychiatric diagnoses should be used.
- More modern forms of psychosurgery are targeted on localised, specific brain areas, and therefore avoid large-scale brain destruction, reducing the risks of irreversible side effects such as personality changes.

**psychological therapies** treatments of anxiety disorders through non-physical means of intervention

**behavioural therapies** treatments of anxiety disorders that seek to modify maladaptive behaviour by the substitution of new responses

### Evaluation: OCD

- Psychosurgery should only be used after a patient has given fully informed consent. However, it is debatable whether a person with severe OCD can actually give fully informed consent, suggesting that there may be ethical problems in administering such a treatment.
- Whether psychosurgery should be used generally involves a cost–benefit analysis, where the possible costs, such as irreversible side effects, are weighed against the possible benefits, such as the lessening of symptoms detrimental to everyday functioning.
- Psychosurgery cannot be considered to be a cure for OCD and patients who undergo it will probably continue to need psychiatric support following the procedure, even if it is considered to be a success.

# Psychological therapies for anxiety disorders

This section discusses the following psychological therapies for anxiety disorders: behavioural therapies, psychodynamic therapies and cognitive behavioural therapy.

## Behavioural therapies

Behaviourism perceives mental disorders as maladaptive behaviours acquired through learning experiences, which can be eradicated and replaced with adaptive behaviours via behavioural therapies.

**Systematic desensitisation** (SD) is the main behaviourist treatment used to combat phobias. Developed by Wolpe (1958), SD is based on classical conditioning, with a patient learning in stages to replace their fear response with feelings of calm and relaxation, so removing the previous association between the phobic object/situation and fear. The central idea is that it is not possible for the two opposing emotions of anxiety and relaxation to exist together at the same time (**reciprocal inhibition**). The treatment uses a progressive, step-by-step approach to the feared object or situation and generally takes about a month to advance through the entire desensitisation hierarchy.

The hierarchy is drawn up before treatment commences, going from the least to the most feared type of contact with the phobic object/situation, and the patient is also taught relaxation strategies to use at each stage of contact. Such contact is usually done by imagining the scenario (**covert desensitisation**), but can sometimes involve actual contact (**in vivo desensitisation**). For example, a patient with a snake phobia may begin SD treatment by looking at a picture of a snake in a sealed tank and progressively work through to actually holding a snake in their hands.

Another behaviourist therapy is that of **implosion** (**flooding**), where instead of a step-by-step approach to the feared object, the patient goes straight to the top of the hierarchy and imagines, or has direct contact with, the most feared scenario. The idea is that the patient is not allowed to make their usual avoidance response and therefore anxiety peaks at such a high level that it cannot be maintained and eventually subsides.

SD is also used as a treatment for OCD, where the sufferer is first taught relaxation strategies and is then introduced to the object or situation that causes their obsession and, by using the relaxation strategies, lowers their anxiety levels.

Another behaviourist treatment for OCD is **exposure and response prevention** (ERP), where sufferers are introduced to the object/situation that causes their obsession, but are not allowed to make their normal obsessive response. The idea is that OCD has occurred through reinforcement and so if anxiety-creating scenarios are avoided, such reinforcement is prevented and relearning can occur. Therefore, if an OCD sufferer who obsessively brushes their drive is prevented from doing so, then they come to realise the obsession that caused their feelings of anxiety is no longer doing so.

### Research: phobic disorders

- Jones (1924) used SD to eradicate 'Little Peter's' phobia of white fluffy animals and objects, for example rabbits and cotton wool. The rabbit was gradually presented to the patient at closer distances each time his anxiety levels subsided enough to permit movement to the next stage. Peter was also given foods he liked so that a positive association was developed with the rabbit. Eventually he developed affection for the rabbit, which was generalised to other similar animals and objects.
- Rothbaum et al. (1998) reported on virtual reality exposure therapy, where patients are active participants within a computer-generated three-dimensional world that changes naturally with head movements. The advantage of this therapy over normal SD and implosion is that treatment can occur without ever leaving the therapist's office, more control is gained over phobic stimuli and there is less exposure of the patient to harm and embarrassment.
- Wolpe (1960) used implosion to remove a girl's phobia of driving in cars. The girl was forced into a car and driven around for 4 hours until her initial hysteria had completely subsided, demonstrating the effectiveness of the treatment.

### Research: OCD

- Gertz (1966) reported that in vivo SD worked well with OCD patients, with 66% of sufferers responding to treatment, suggesting it is effective.
- Lindsay et al. (1997) randomly assigned 18 OCD patients to either ERP or anxiety management programmes. After 3 weeks there was a significant reduction in symptoms for the ERP patients, but not for those on the anxiety management programmes, implying that symptom reduction is a result of the specific techniques of exposure and response prevention.
- Baer (1991) introduced a self-directed, step-by-step form of ERP that is equally as effective for mild forms of OCD as seeing a therapist and can therefore be considered very cost-effective.

## Evaluation: phobic disorders

- SD is mainly suitable for those patients who are able to learn and use relaxation strategies and have imaginations vivid enough to conjure up images of their feared object/situation.
- Although a patient may be able to gradually confront their phobia in an imaginary sense, there is no guarantee that this will work with the actual object/situation, which is probably why in vivo treatment is perceived as being superior to covert desensitisation.
- There are ethical considerations to take into account with both SD and implosion, as both can be seen as psychologically harmful, though a cost–benefit analysis may regard the short-term cost of distress as being outweighed by the benefit of eradicating the phobia.

**Examiner tip**

In questions requiring an evaluation of a therapy (or an explanation of a disorder), take care to use research evidence to directly evaluate the therapy/explanation and not merely provide general methodological criticism of the study, for example that the study is an experiment and therefore shows causality, lacks ecological validity etc. Instead, say how it supports the therapy/explanation.

### Evaluation: OCD

- ERP can have large drop-out rates due to the high levels of anxiety it produces, and it is therefore usually combined with drug treatment so that anxiety levels can be controlled.
- ERP can be considered more effective than drug treatments as relapse rates are much lower, suggesting ERP brings long-term, lasting benefits.
- Even patients with long-lasting and severe OCD symptoms can benefit from ERP treatment as long as they are suitably motivated to get well. However, the treatment is seen as less effective for patients who do not exhibit overt compulsions and those with moderate to severe depression.

## Psychodynamic therapies

**psychodynamic therapies** treatment of anxiety disorders that aims to gain insight into the unconscious mind to reduce psychic tension

Psychodynamic therapies have their origins in Freud's psychoanalytic theory and come in varying forms. Psychoanalysis is an intensive form, consisting of several sessions a week for lengthy periods, traditionally conducted with the patient lying on a couch. Psychoanalytic psychotherapy is a less intensive form, consisting of fewer sessions per week and over a shorter period, with therapist and patient in a face-to-face scenario.

Psychodynamic therapies try to reveal the repressed conflicts that are expressed as phobias so that the sufferer can have insight into the origins of their disorder and eventually arrive at a more rational understanding of events that occurred in their childhood.

Before the introduction of other types of treatments and therapies, psychoanalysis was often used as a treatment for OCD, and indeed it can be considered a useful means of addressing the condition, as often sufferers do have a degree of insight into their condition.

#### Research: phobic disorders

- Freud (1909) presented the case study of 'Little Hans', a 5-year-old boy with a fear of being bitten by a horse, which was interpreted as an unconscious fear of his father. By gaining insight into his condition and dealing with the underlying issues, it was claimed that Hans's phobia had been cured, suggesting that the psychodynamic therapies do have value.
- Knijnik et al. (2004) gave psychodynamic group therapy (PGT) for 12 weeks to patients with social phobias and found their condition improved, lending support to the psychodynamic explanation.
- Klein et al. (1983) reported that psychodynamic therapy for specific phobias was equally as effective as in vivo behaviourist treatments after 26 weeks of treatment, indicating the worth of psychodynamic-based treatments.

**Research: OCD**

- Malan (1979) reported that psychodynamic therapies have had little success with OCD, because when obsessional symptoms are treated by psychotherapy, patients become conscious of their inner conflicts but therapeutic improvements do not follow.
- Gava et al. (2009) attempted to evaluate different biological and psychological treatments for OCD by reviewing studies that compared treatments. Cognitive and behavioural treatments were found to be superior, but the researchers were unable to properly assess psychodynamic treatments due to a lack of evidence, suggesting the treatment has become obsolete.
- Greist and Jefferson (2007) reported that psychodynamic psychotherapy and psychoanalysis have generally not been effective for people with OCD, weakening support for such treatments.

**Knowledge check 36**

What does research suggest about the effectiveness of (a) behavioural therapies and (b) psychodynamic therapies as treatments for phobias and OCD?

## Evaluation: phobic disorders

- The psychodynamic approach to treating phobias can work in association with cognitive and humanistic as well as behavioural and social therapies, demonstrating its flexibility and range of use.
- Psychodynamic therapies are suitable for use with children, adolescents and adults.
- Psychodynamic therapies may be more suitable for certain types of patient, such as those who have insight into their condition and who have the verbal skills to express themselves to a therapist.

## Evaluation: OCD

- Although psychoanalysis seems an appropriate treatment for OCD because sufferers often have insight into their condition, insight alone may not be enough to eradicate the disorder, as evidence suggests it to be largely biological in nature.
- Psychodynamic therapies are not considered to be a cost-effective form of treatment, due to their lengthy nature, reliance on trained therapists and high drop-out rates.
- Unlike cognitive behavioural therapies that have been developed solely for OCD sufferers, there are no psychodynamic treatments designed specifically to combat the disorder.

# Cognitive behavioural therapy (CBT)

CBT is the most frequently used treatment for phobias and OCD, which is in itself a testament to its effectiveness. Treatments generally occur once every 7 to 14 days for about 15 sessions in total.

The general aim of CBT is to help patients identify irrational and maladaptive thinking patterns and change them to rational, adaptive ones. Thinking is seen as underpinning feelings and behaviour, so if modes of thinking are changed, feelings and behaviour should also change for the better. Sometimes the drawing of diagrams

**cognitive behavioural therapy (CBT)** treatment of anxiety disorders that attempts to modify thought patterns to alter behavioural and emotional states

that demonstrate links between thinking, emotions and behaviour is used to facilitate this process.

Therefore, for a patient with a snake phobia the therapist will first get the phobic to express their beliefs about snakes and then challenge these beliefs with rational arguments. Then the patient may be encouraged to successfully interact with snakes and record details of the experience so that they can be referred back to if the sufferer returns to their irrational beliefs.

One specific form of CBT used with phobics is **cognitive behavioural group therapy** (CBGT), where other group members support sufferers as they work through a hierarchy of fears, using relaxation strategies at each step. The cognitive element of the treatment involves replacing irrational beliefs that generate anxiety with rational ones. Phobic situations are enacted, with group members challenging each other's irrational beliefs.

With OCD, CBT is oriented towards changing obsessional thinking, such as in **habituation training** (HT), where sufferers relive obsessional thoughts repeatedly in order to reduce the anxiety created.

### Research: phobic disorders

- Spence et al. (2000) assessed the value of CBT in treating 50 children aged between 7 and 14 with social phobias. Child-focused CBT and CBT plus parental involvement were found to be effective in reducing social and general anxiety levels and these improvements were retained at a 1-year follow-up, suggesting CBT to have a long-term effectiveness with phobic children.
- Kvale et al. (2004) conducted a meta-analysis of 38 treatment studies for people with dental phobias, finding that CBT resulted in 77% of patients regularly visiting a dentist 4 years after treatment.
- Holmberg et al. (2006) assessed the value of CBT in treating patients with phobic postural vertigo, where sufferers become anxious and dizzy when standing or walking, a condition that seriously hampers normal everyday functioning. They found that CBT had a limited long-term effect, but that the condition was much harder to treat than other phobias, suggesting CBT may be more appropriate with certain phobic disorders than others.

### Research: OCD

- O'Kearney et al. (2006) assessed the ability of CBT to treat children and adolescents under the age of 18 with OCD, finding it effective, but more so when combined with drug treatments.
- Sousa et al. (2007) used 56 adults with OCD to compare group CBT with the SSRI antidepressant drug sertraline over a period of 12 weeks. They found that group CBT led more frequently to complete remission of OCD symptoms than drug treatment, demonstrating CBT's superiority.
- Vogel et al. (1992) investigated the effectiveness of habituation training in treating patients suffering from OCD, finding declines in obsessional thinking within sessions but not between sessions, which implies that the technique is of little value in the real world.

**Examiner tip**

Always read questions carefully, as they detail the exact requirements. For example, if a question asks for an outline of one psychological therapy and more than one is provided, only the best one is credited. Conversely, if a question asks for an outline of two therapies and only one is given, then, however detailed and accurate, marks will be limited.

**Knowledge check 37**

What does research suggest about the effectiveness of CBT as a treatment for phobias and OCD?

## Evaluation: phobic disorders

- There may be long-term benefits to CBT, as the techniques used to combat phobias can be used continually to help stop symptoms returning.
- For CBT to be effective, training is essential, successful treatment being dependent upon developing empathy, respect, unconditional positive regard and honesty between patient and practitioner.
- One of the advantages of CBT compared to other forms of treatment is that it produces little in the way of side effects.

## Evaluation: OCD

- The chances of CBT being successful are highly correlated with the strength of the working relationship created between therapist and patient, indicating the pivotal role that the therapist plays in the administering of the treatment.
- Suitably trained nurses have proven as effective as psychiatrists and psychologists in treating patients with OCD, demonstrating the simplicity of the treatment and its cost-effectiveness.
- One problem with CBT, as with all 'talking therapies', is that it might not be suitable for those patients who have difficulties discussing their inner feelings, or for those who do not possess the verbal skills to do so.

**Summary**

- Phobias are extreme, irrational, enduring fears, while OCD consists of persistent, intrusive thoughts that can occur as both obsessions and compulsions. Both are diagnosable by symptoms and classed as anxiety disorders when they prevent normal day-to-day functioning.
- Both phobias and OCD have shown reliability of diagnosis, but both have issues concerning validity of diagnosis.
- Biological explanations include roles for genetics, evolution and biochemistry.
- Psychological explanations focus on behaviourist learning experiences, as well as psychodynamic, cognitive and sociocultural factors.
- The main biological treatment of phobias and OCD are drug therapies, with ECT also used against severe, resistant cases of both disorders.
- Psychological treatments for phobias and OCD include behavioural and psychodynamic therapies and the more favoured cognitive behavioural therapy (CBT).

# Questions & Answers

This section contains mark band descriptors and sample questions in the style of Unit 4. Each question is accompanied by guidance explaining the question's requirements, followed by a sample answer and examiner's comments and marks, detailing the strengths and weaknesses of each answer and explaining how the marks were awarded. Examiner's comments are preceded by the icon 🅔.

# The examination

The Unit 4 examination lasts 2 hours and there will be three sections: A, B and C. In Section A (Psychopathology) there will be three questions from which you must select and answer one. In Section B (Psychology in Action) there will be three questions from which you must select and answer one. In Section C (Psychological Research and Scientific Method) there will be one compulsory structured question.

Each question in sections A and B is worth 24 marks overall, although some questions may be split into parts. The compulsory question in Section C is worth 30 marks.

To ensure that you can answer a question in Section A, you must study and revise all the subject content listed in the specification for either schizophrenia, depression or anxiety disorders (for the latter, either phobic disorders or obsessive–compulsive disorder). To ensure that you can answer a question in Section B, you must study and revise all the subject content listed in the specification for either media psychology, the psychology of addictive behaviour or anomalistic psychology. To ensure that you can answer the compulsory structured question in Section C, you must study and revise all the subject content listed in the specification for psychological research and scientific method.

This paper will account for 50% of the total A2 marks and 25% of the total A-level. You may sit this examination in either January or June of each year.

## Assessment objectives

In this psychology examination three sets of skills or assessment objectives are tested: AO1, AO2 and AO3.

**AO1** (assessment objective 1) concerns questions designed to test your knowledge and understanding of psychological theories, terminology, concepts, studies and methods. You should be able to:
- recognise, recall and show understanding of knowledge
- select, organise and communicate relevant information in a variety of forms
- present and organise material clearly
- use relevant psychological terminology

**AO2** (assessment objective 2) concerns questions designed to test your knowledge and understanding and the application of knowledge via analysis and evaluation of psychological theories, concepts, studies and methods. You should be able to:
- analyse and evaluate knowledge and processes
- apply knowledge and processes to novel situations, including those relating to issues
- assess the validity, reliability and credibility of information

**AO3** (assessment objective 3) concerns questions designed to test your knowledge and application of knowledge and your understanding of how psychology as a science works. You should be able to:
- describe ethical, safe and skilful practical techniques and processes and the appropriate selection of qualitative and quantitative methods
- know how to make, record and communicate reliable and valid observations and measurements with appropriate accuracy and precision, through using primary and secondary sources
- analyse, interpret, explain and evaluate the methodology, results and impact of experimental and investigative activities in a variety of ways

For each question in sections A and B there are 8 AO1 marks, 12 AO2 marks and 4 AO3 marks. For the compulsory structured question in Section C there are 2 AO1 marks, 3 AO2 marks and 25 AO3 marks.

# Good practice

**For AO1** you should:
- avoid 'storytelling' or 'common-sense' answers that lack psychological content
- give some depth to your answers and not just provide a list of points
- achieve a balance between the breadth and depth of your answer
- make your answer coherent; it should be clearly written and have a continuity to it so that it does not read as a series of unconnected comments

**For AO2/AO3** you should:
- elaborate upon evaluative points in order to construct an effective commentary
- where possible and appropriate, make use of both negative and positive criticism, for example, methodological faults and practical applications
- draw conclusions and interpretations from your AO1 material
- select material carefully so that it is specifically directed at the question, rather than just forming a general answer on the topic area
- avoid overuse of generic evaluation, such as the repetitive detailing of methodological strengths and weaknesses of all research studies included in your answer
- present arguments and evaluations with clarity
- ensure that you have included within your evaluation and analysis evidence of synopticity

# How the marks are awarded

## AO1 mark band descriptors (4 marks)

| | |
|---|---|
| **4 marks** | Outline is reasonably thorough, accurate and coherent. |
| **3–2 marks** | Outline is limited, generally accurate and reasonably coherent. |
| **1 mark** | Outline is weak and muddled. |
| **0 marks** | No creditworthy material is apparent. |

## AO1 mark band descriptors (8 marks)

| | |
|---|---|
| **8 marks** | **Sound**<br>Knowledge and understanding are accurate and well detailed.<br>A good range of relevant material has been presented.<br>There is substantial evidence of breadth/depth.<br>Organisation and structure of the answer are coherent. |
| **7–5 marks** | **Reasonable**<br>Knowledge and understanding are generally accurate and reasonably detailed.<br>A range of relevant material has been presented.<br>There is evidence of breadth and/or depth.<br>Organisation and structure of the answer are reasonably coherent. |
| **4–3 marks** | **Basic**<br>Knowledge and understanding are basic/relatively superficial.<br>A restricted range of material has been presented.<br>Organisation and structure of the answer are basic. |
| **2–1 marks** | **Rudimentary**<br>Knowledge and understanding are rudimentary and may be muddled and/or inaccurate.<br>The material presented may be brief or largely irrelevant.<br>The answer lacks organisation and structure. |
| **0 marks** | No creditworthy material is apparent. |

## AO2/AO3 mark band descriptors (16 marks)

| | |
|---|---|
| **16–13 marks** | **Effective**<br>Evaluation shows sound analysis and understanding.<br>Answer is well focused and displays coherent elaboration and/or a clear line of argument is apparent.<br>Effective use is made of issues/debates/approaches.<br>There is substantial evidence of synopticity.<br>Well-structured ideas are expressed clearly and fluently.<br>There is consistent effective use of psychological terminology and appropriate use of grammar, spelling and punctuation. |

| 12–9 marks | **Reasonable** |
|---|---|
| | Evaluation shows reasonable analysis and understanding. |
| | Answer is generally focused and displays reasonable elaboration and/or a line of argument is apparent. |
| | A reasonably effective use is made of issues/debates/approaches. |
| | There is evidence of synopticity. |
| | Most ideas are appropriately structured and expressed clearly. |
| | There is appropriate use of psychological terminology and there are some minor errors of grammar; spelling and punctuation only occasionally compromise meaning. |
| 8–5 marks | **Basic** |
| | Evaluation and analysis show basic, superficial understanding. |
| | Answer is sometimes focused and has some evidence of elaboration. |
| | There is a superficial use of issues/debates/approaches. |
| | There is some evidence of synopticity. |
| | The expression of ideas lacks clarity. |
| | There is limited use of psychological terminology and errors of grammar, spelling and punctuation are intrusive. |
| 4–1 marks | **Rudimentary** |
| | Evaluation and analysis are rudimentary, showing very limited understanding. |
| | Answer is weak, muddled and incomplete. |
| | Material is not used effectively and may be mainly irrelevant. |
| | Any reference to issues/debates/approaches is muddled or inaccurate. |
| | There is little or no evidence of synopticity. |
| | The expression of ideas is deficient, demonstrating confusion and ambiguity. |
| | The answer lacks structure and may be just a series of unconnected points. |
| | There are errors in grammar, spelling and punctuation that are frequent and intrusive. |
| 0 marks | No creditworthy material is evident. |

# Explanation of examination injunctions

## AO1

**Outline:** provide brief details without explanation

**Describe:** provide a detailed account without explanation

## AO2

**Evaluate:** assess the value/effectiveness

**Discuss:** provide a reasoned, balanced account

# Question 1 **Schizophrenia (I)**

**Discuss biological explanations of schizophrenia.**                    (24 marks)

ⓔ This is a straightforward essay question taken directly from the specification. Material on at least two biological explanations must be given; if more than two explanations are offered, less detail would be expected. There are 8 marks available for describing biological explanations, leaving 16 marks for the evaluation, with a wealth of research evidence available to use. Material on psychological explanations would not gain credit if used descriptively but could form part of an evaluation as a comparison to biological explanations.

## Student answer

One biological explanation of schizophrenia is the genetic explanation **a** with evidence from twin, family and adoption studies being used to indicate whether schizophrenia has a genetic component. Recently gene mapping studies **a** have been performed that compare genetic material from families with a high and low incidence of the disorder to assess whether several genes rather than a single one are at work to produce increased vulnerability to developing schizophrenia.

Support for the genetic argument was provided by Gottesman and Shields (1976) **c**, who reviewed five twin studies to find a concordance rate of up to 91% between MZ identical twins with severe forms of schizophrenia, implying genetics to have a bigger influence on chronic schizophrenia. This was backed up by Kety and Ingraham (1992) **c d**, who identified schizophrenics who had been adopted and compared the incidence of the condition among their adoptive and biological relatives: they found the rate of schizophrenia to be ten times higher among biological relatives, implying genes to play a much larger role than environmental factors. However, Leo (2006) **d** argues Kety and Ingraham's evidence to be suspect **e**, as sample sizes were small, making generalisation difficult, and **e** many of the biological relatives were rather distant ones, such as half-siblings, and therefore of low biological similarity.

Twin studies have not gone without criticism either **d**; they may suggest a genetic influence, but often do not consider the influence of social class and socio-psychological factors between twins. Furthermore, Hedgecoe (2001) **d f** argues that scientists have tried to construct schizophrenia as a genetic disease by using evidence from twin and adoption studies in a biased way to create a narrative about schizophrenia that subtly prioritises genetic explanations.

A second biological explanation is provided by the evolutionary perspective **b**, which believes that, as the disorder continues to be represented in the population and historical records show it to have been around for a long time, then it must have an adaptive value and serve a beneficial purpose. If the condition were maladaptive then the process of natural selection would have worked to remove it from the gene pool. Stevens and Price (1997) formulated the group splitting hypothesis **b**, where dynamic leaders with schizophrenic-like qualities of high energy, delusions of grandeur and an apparent ability to communicate with 'higher beings' are required when groups split after reaching a critical size for a given environment.

Support for the evolutionary viewpoint comes from Peters et al. (1999) **c**, who studied religious cults and found their leaders to be charismatic and to hold near-psychotic delusional beliefs, suggesting that schizophrenic traits do play a role in the splitting and dispersal of people. This is backed up by Polimeni and Reiss (2002) **c d**, who propose that schizophrenia evolved because its characteristics, such as communicating with spirits, enhanced a spiritual group leader's ability to perform religious ceremonies, suggesting that schizophrenia served as a behavioural specialisation in the EEA. However **d**, although some leaders may exhibit schizophrenic traits, the majority do not, even in new breakaway group factions, weakening support for the theory somewhat. Furthermore **d**, evolutionary theory is difficult to test **f**, as evidence tends to be retrospective and lacking in empirical support.

🄴 This is an excellent answer in all respects. First, the requirements of the question are completely met; two biological explanations, **a** genetics and **b** evolution, are outlined clearly, accurately and concisely, with no irrelevant material included, and these are then **c** thoroughly evaluated in terms of appropriate research evidence. **d** Evaluative points are made in a fashion that allows them to be constructed into an elaborated and effective commentary, with the inclusion also of **e** some material relating to relevant issues and **f** methodological points.

The balance between descriptive and evaluative material is also excellent, with a preference for evaluative material, where most of the marks are available. Finally, the construction of the answer is very sound, with the student choosing to outline one explanation first and then evaluate it, followed by the outlining and evaluation of the second explanation.

**(AO1 = 8/8) + (AO2/AO3 = 16/16) = 24/24 marks**

## Question 2 **Schizophrenia (II)**

| | |
|---|---|
| **(a) Outline the clinical characteristics of schizophrenia.** | (8 marks) |
| **(b) Evaluate the extent to which diagnoses of schizophrenia are reliable and valid.** | (16 marks) |

🄴 This type of parted question places the descriptive part of the question in one section and the evaluative in the other. Therefore in part (a) only descriptive material should be offered relating to clinical characteristics of schizophrenia — no marks are earned for including evaluative material. Part (b) requires an evaluation of how reliable and valid diagnoses of schizophrenia are, and any purely descriptive material placed in this section would gain no credit.

### Student answer

**(a)** For a person to be diagnosed as schizophrenic, two or more symptoms must be apparent for at least a month **a** along with reduced social functioning **a**. There are a number of clinical characteristics of schizophrenia, such as passivity experiences and thought disorders **a**, where thoughts and actions are seen as under external control, or being inserted, withdrawn or broadcast to others; also auditory hallucinations **a**, where voices inside the head give a running commentary, or discuss the sufferer's behaviour.

Primary delusions usually occur, with delusions of grandeur coming first **a**, where the sufferer thinks they're someone important, and then later delusions of persecution **a**, where they believe someone is out to get them. Thought process disorders can be apparent **a**, where sufferers wander off the point, muddle their words, or invent new words and phrases.

Disturbances of affect occur **a**, where sufferers appear indifferent, display inappropriate emotional responses, or exhibit big mood swings. Psychomotor disturbances may also be apparent **a**, where sufferers go into statue-like poses or exhibit tics, twitches and repetitive behaviours. Finally, sufferers may have a lack of volition **a**, where they are unable to make decisions, lack motivation and do not show affection.

ⓔ This is excellent: it is full of a clinical characteristics **a** that are relevant and accurately described, with the length just right to gain the marks on offer and for the time available. The list-like quality of the answer is fine, as it fits the requirements of this question.

**(b)** Schizophrenia involves the loss of unity to one's personality **a** and most commonly occurs between 15 and 45 years of age **a**, with an equal number of males and females **a**, though males tend to develop the disorder at an earlier age **a**.

Reliability refers to the consistency of measurements and affects diagnoses in two ways **b**: first, test–retest reliability **b**, where a clinician makes similar, consistent diagnoses of a patient on different occasions, and second, inter-rater reliability **b**, where several clinicians make identical, but independent, diagnoses of the same patient.

Validity refers to how accurate, meaningful and useful diagnoses are **c** and there are a number of ways in which validity can be assessed, but first a diagnosis must be reliable to be valid, though being reliable is no guarantee of validity **ab**. Predictive validity **c** occurs when diagnosis leads to successful treatment of the disorder, while descriptive validity **c** occurs when patients diagnosed with different disorders actually do differ from each other. There is also aetiological validity **c**, where diagnosed schizophrenics should have the same cause for their disorder.

Beck (1962) **d** found a 54% concordance rate between the diagnoses of experienced clinicians, while Söderberg (2005) **d** found one of 81%, suggesting diagnoses have become more reliable over time. Nilsson (2000) **d** found a 60% concordance rate between clinicians using the ICD classification system, which suggests the DSM system **e** is more reliable.

Hollis (2000) **d** applied DSM classification diagnoses to 93 sets of patient case notes and found the diagnosis of schizophrenia had a high level of stability, indicating the diagnoses to be mainly valid.

Bottas (2009) **d** found that 1% of the population is schizophrenic and 3% suffer from obsessive–compulsive disorder (OCD), but the incidence of schizophrenia with OCD is higher than probability would suggest, which seems to indicate a separate schizo-obsessive disorder may exist, implying that separate types of schizophrenia may exist.

**e** This answer has many faults. First, **a** the student seems to feel the need to provide descriptive details of schizophrenia, which the question does not call for. Then more time is wasted gaining no marks, by describing what **b** reliability and **c** validity are, when what the question requires is an evaluative assessment of whether diagnoses of schizophrenia actually are reliable and valid. The student finally gets round to doing this in the second half of the answer, where **d** relevant research is introduced and used in an evaluative manner. However, this part of the answer lacks a little clarity: for instance, **e** it is not made very clear why DSM classification should be considered more valid than the ICD one. Additionally, the evaluative points that are made do not really link together well to form any sort of elaborated discussion.

**(a) (AOI = (8/8) + (b) (AO2/AO3 = 6/16) = 14/24 marks**

# Question 3 **Schizophrenia (III)**

**(a) Outline one biological therapy for the treatment of schizophrenia.**                     (4 marks)

**e** Part (a) requires only descriptive material relating to one biological therapy for the treatment of schizophrenia, so any evaluative material produced here will not gain credit. If more than one biological therapy were to be offered, all would be marked, but only the best one would be credited.

### Student answer

**(a)** The main biological treatment for schizophrenia is antipsychotic drugs **a**. These drugs do not cure the disorder **b**, but dampen down symptoms so that a normal level of functioning is possible. Typical antipsychotics like chlorpromazine **a**, work by blocking the receptors in synapses that absorb dopamine, thus reducing positive symptoms such as auditory hallucinations **b**. Atypical antipsychotics, such as clozapine **a**, were introduced in the 1990s **b** and act upon serotonin and dopamine production, affecting negative symptoms such as reduced emotional expression. Some patients only have to take one course of antipsychotics, while others have to take a regular dose to prevent symptoms reappearing. Others do not respond at all **b**.

**e** The first part of this answer is very good; **a** it has relevant and accurate content, **b** as well as being fairly detailed.

**(b) Outline and evaluate psychological therapies as treatments of schizophrenia.**    (20 marks)

ⓔ Part (b) requires both descriptive and evaluative material, this time relating to psychological therapies. Material on at least two psychological therapies must be given; if more than two are covered, less detail would be expected.

**(b)** One behaviourist treatment of schizophrenia is token economies **a**, where a change in behaviour is gained by giving tokens, which can be exchanged for goods or privileges, immediately after a patient exhibits desired actions. Token economy **a c** is designed to increase motivation, attention and social participation of patients. McMonagle and Sultana (2000) **d** reviewed token economy regimes, finding support for the treatment as they did reduce symptoms, though it was not clear **e** if this was maintained beyond the treatment programme. Further support **e** came from Upper and Newton (1971) **d**, finding that the weight gain associated with taking antipsychotics could be reduced by 3 pounds a week by using token economy. However **e**, token economy, even with its good record, has fallen out of favour, due to staff resistance, economic restraints, more use of community-based treatments and legal and ethical challenges to its use.

Another psychological treatment for schizophrenia is cognitive behavioural therapy (CBT) **b c**, which is the most commonly used psychological treatment for the disorder. The central idea behind the treatment **b** is that beliefs, expectations and cognitive assessments of self, the environment and the nature of personal problems affect how a person views others and themselves, how problems are dealt with and how good a person is at coping and reaching goals. CBT **b c** is designed to address the distorted perceptions and disordered thoughts that are typical of the disorder, and is often used in tandem with a course of antipsychotic drugs that reduce psychotic thought processes down to a level where psychological treatments, such as CBT, can be used. CBT **b c** is used about once a week, for between 5 and 15 sessions, to identify the links between thoughts, behaviour and feelings. The idea is that comprehension of where symptoms originate from is useful in reducing anxiety levels.

Turkington (2006) **d** provided support for CBT by finding it to be highly effective and to be recommended as a mainstream treatment. Trower (2004) **d** supplied further support **e** by finding that CBT reduces positive and negative symptoms and brings a better quality of life, though CBT **e** is not a replacement for medication and is not suitable for everyone. Tarrier (2005) **d** also supported the use of CBT **e** by finding it reduces symptoms and has a low relapse rate, but this support was weakened **e** by the fact that the treatment was only shown to be effective in the short term.

CBT is not suitable for everyone **e**, especially not for those who refuse medication or are too thought-disorientated, too agitated or too paranoid to form a trusting alliance with a practitioner.

ⓔ The material supplied for this part of this answer is relevant, accurate and cohesive. However, for the marks available, the answer is unbalanced. The student addresses the requirement of the question to supply material on more than one psychological therapy, making reference to **a** token

AQA(A) A2 Psychology

economy and **b** CBT but as there are only 4 marks available for **c** the descriptive content, the student provides more than enough material, meaning of course that valuable time is wasted that could have been spent on creating evaluative content. The **d** evaluation of the therapies is of a good quality, it links together well, **e** and the points made are often built upon each other in an effective manner — but the fact remains that there just is not enough of this material to earn the higher levels of the marks available.

**(a) (AOI = 4/4) + (b) (AOI = 4/4) + (AO2/AO3 = 10/16) = 18/24 marks**

# Question 4 **Depression (I)**

**Discuss psychological explanations of depression.**                          (24 marks)

(e)  This is a straightforward essay question taken directly from the specification. Material on at least two psychological explanations must be given; if more than two explanations are offered, less detail would be expected. There are 8 marks available for describing psychological explanations, leaving 16 marks for the evaluation, with a wealth of research evidence available to use. Material on biological explanations would not gain credit if used descriptively, but could form part of an evaluation as a comparison to psychological explanations.

**Student answer**

One psychological explanation of depression is the psychodynamic one **a** that originated with Freud (1917) **d**. He saw depression as being related to melancholic childhood experiences of loss or rejection within one's family. Therefore adulthood depression was a form of delayed regret for such a loss. In this view, a child is unable to express the anger they feel over their loss and so represses it, directing it inwards, lowering their self-esteem. Similarly occurring loss or rejection in adulthood could also cause a person to re-experience their childhood loss. Bowlby (1973) offers a similar view **d**, whereby children experiencing separation from a mother figure in early childhood could develop an enhanced vulnerability to experiencing depression in later life.

Swaffer and Hollin (2001) **e** supported the psychodynamic viewpoint, when finding that young offenders who repressed anger had an increased vulnerability to developing depression. However, Abela (2007) **f** found that children who were high on dependency showed no increases in hopelessness or depression following negative life events, reducing support for the model. A strength **e** of the psychodynamic model is that it can explain the physical features of depression as well as psychological ones. For instance **f**, the lack of energy often associated with depression is seen as due to the amount of energy expended in keeping anger repressed.

Another psychological explanation is that in terms of sociocultural factors **b**, such as the family and social influences **d**. The view here is that stressors in the form of life events can play a pivotal role in the onset and maintenance of depression. Therefore those who have reduced social support and experience stressful life events are more vulnerable to developing depression and then staying depressed for prolonged periods. This means that individuals who lack social and interpersonal skills will also be more vulnerable to becoming depressed.

Support for this view comes from Cox (2007) **e**, who found that East African mothers who did not participate in traditional post-natal rituals experienced reduced self-esteem and stressful marital relationships, leading to ambivalent social status and an increased risk of experiencing post-natal depression. Further support **e f** comes from Takaaki (2003), who found that the incidence of unipolar depression in Japan had increased dramatically and that this was related to changes in family and social environments, such as the movement of younger people to urban environments, collapsing traditional family structures. This then led to an increase in stressful life events and a lack of family support to deal with such stressors, therefore fitting the sociocultural explanation of depression.

A third type of psychological explanation for depression is that of the behaviourist outlook **c**, where depression is seen as a learned condition and therefore not as a mental illness. Lewinsohn (1974) **c** believes depression can occur due to a decline in positive reinforcement after, for example, a breakdown in a romantic relationship, leading to fewer opportunities for experiencing enjoyable outcomes. This could lead to a cycle of social withdrawal that prolongs the depression.

Behaviourism can also explain depression as occurring through learned helplessness **c**, where individuals learn that they seemingly cannot influence events (for instance, being unemployed and applying for lots of jobs, but not even getting one interview), leading to a loss of motivation and eventually depression. Depression may also occur in the form of operant conditioning **c**, where reinforcements occur as the attention and sympathy other people give to the sufferer.

**e** Three appropriate psychological explanations are offered, relating to **a** the psychodynamic approach, **b** sociocultural factors and **c** the behaviourist approach, and although **d** each is accurately and coherently outlined, providing material on just two explanations would probably have been a better idea, as too much descriptive material is included for the 8 AO1 marks available. This takes away from the amount of time the student had to produce an evaluation of these explanations — indeed, no evaluation of the behaviourist viewpoint is offered at all, presumably because the student did not have enough time to do so.

The **e** evaluative material that is offered is **f** relevant, well expressed, reasonably detailed and built up into a fairly effective commentary. However, the fact remains that, if the student had constructed the answer better and given more consideration to the selection of material, a higher mark would have been gained.

**(AO1 = 8/8) + (AO2/AO3 = 8/16) = 16/24 marks**

# Question 5 Depression (II)

| | |
|---|---|
| **(a) Outline the clinical characteristics of depression.** | (8 marks) |
| **(b) To what extent are diagnoses of depression reliable and valid?** | (16 marks) |

(e) This type of parted question places the descriptive part of the question in one section and the evaluative in the other. Therefore, in part (a) only descriptive material should be offered relating to clinical characteristics of depression — no marks are earned for including evaluative material. Part (b) requires an evaluation of how reliable and valid diagnoses of depression are, and any purely descriptive material placed in this section gains no credit.

**Student answer**

**(a)** Depression is a mood disorder that about 20% of people will suffer, with women twice as susceptible. It can occur in cycles, generally lasting between 4 and 6 months, and incurs a discernible suicide risk. DSM-IV lists the clinical characteristics of the disorder **a**, of which at least five must be apparent every day for 2 weeks for someone to be diagnosed as depressive, with a breakdown in everyday functioning also evident **a**.

Symptoms include a constant depressed mood (either reported by the sufferer or observed by others), also a lessened interest in daily activities, plus weight loss or decrease in appetite. There can also be sleep pattern disturbance, either insomnia or oversleeping, plus fatigue, lethargy or agitation **b**. Other symptoms are reduced concentration, where the sufferer has difficulty paying attention, slowed-down thinking and indecisiveness, plus worthlessness, where constant feelings of reduced worth and inappropriate guilt are experienced, and maybe a focus on death, where constant thoughts of death and suicide are apparent **b**.

Depression can also occur as two broad types **c**. The first is unipolar or major depression **c**, which occurs simply as a cycle of depression. The second is bipolar or manic depression **c**, where a sufferer goes from being highly aroused and excited, often experiencing delusions and hallucinations, to having major depressive episodes.

(e) This answer is exceedingly good; it is written in an informative yet concise style and contains a wealth of accurate, relevant and sufficiently **a** detailed information concerning general characteristics, **b** symptoms and **c** subtypes. The amount of content is quite sufficient to earn all the 8 marks on offer.

**(b)** Reliability concerns the consistency of depression diagnoses, while validity concerns their accuracy. Making reliable diagnoses of depression is problematic, as such decisions have to be made mainly on patient-reported symptoms, rather than physical signs as with medical disorders; and even with physical medical disorders, reliable diagnoses do not always occur **a c**. Furthermore, most people's moods vary over time, so again it is hard to know when a person is clinically depressed rather than just down, though the modern requirement for symptoms to be present for some time has aided the diagnostic process **a c**. Another problem in diagnosis **a** is taking into consideration the degree to which a person is depressed **c**. Diagnosis used to be performed mainly by clinical interviews, but increasingly use has been made of depression inventories to diagnose the disorder, and reliability has been improved.

Enfield (2002) **b** found a high rate of agreement between skilled clinicians in diagnosing depression, implying a high degree of inter-rater reliability **c**, but also emphasising **b** the importance of using expert practitioners. Moca (2007) **b** not only found evidence of similar high rates of inter-rater reliability, 88%, between clinicians, but also a 78% concordance rate for test–retest reliability **c**, which also shows diagnoses to be reliable over time. These figures **b**, although impressive, are lower than those for schizophrenia, suggesting room for improvement. Contrarily, Baca-Garcia (2007) **b**, reviewing an impressive 2,300 diagnoses of patients assessed at least ten times each, found a lower concordance rate for test–retest reliability **c** of only 55%, suggesting that reliability of diagnosis is relatively poor.

Van Weel-Baumgarten (2000) **b** found evidence that validity **d** of diagnosis in the Netherlands was good, with 28 out of 33 depressives being correctly diagnosed using DSM criteria. This was backed up by Sanchez-Villegas (2008) **c**, who used the Structured Clinical Interview and found that over 74% of patients diagnosed with depression had been accurately diagnosed. Almeida and Almeida (1999) **c** also found supportive evidence of validity in depression diagnoses among 64 elderly Australians, using the Geriatric Depression Scale with both ICD and DSM criteria: it was found to be highly valid **d**, though not very useful in assessing the severity of depression. Contrary evidence was reported by Zigler and Phillips (1961) **c**, who found that symptoms of depression were equally likely to be found among neurotic patients as those with bipolar disorder, as well as in 25% of diagnosed schizophrenics, implying a low diagnostic validity **d**.

ⓔ An impressive answer is given, again written very concisely, with a wealth of accurate and relevant evaluative material. **a** The answer begins with evaluative material concerning the difficulty of making reliable diagnoses before moving on to **b** using research evidence in an informative manner that indicates a high-level understanding. The student also evaluates both **c** reliability and **d** validity and although there is more emphasis on reliability, this is not penalised, as there is no requirement to deal with each in a completely balanced fashion.

**(a) (AO1 = 8/8) + (b) (AO2/AO3 = 16/16) = 24/24 marks**

## Question 6 Depression (III)

**(a) Outline one psychological therapy for the treatment of depression.** (4 marks)

ⓔ This question requires only descriptive material relating to one psychological therapy for the treatment of depression, so any evaluative material produced here will not gain credit. If more than one psychological therapy were to be offered, all would be marked, but only the best one would be credited.

**Student answer**

**(a)** The most common treatment for depression is antidepressant drugs **a** and these generally work by stimulating the production of monoamine neurotransmitters in the brain, which increases arousal levels. Monoamine oxidase inhibitors (MAOIs) **a** are an older type of antidepressants that prevent the neurotransmitters serotonin, dopamine and noradrenaline from being broken down, resulting in their levels being increased. Tricyclics **a**, on the other hand, stop serotonin and noradrenaline being reabsorbed, so that again levels are increased. Both these types of drugs are regarded as being effective, but can have side effects, such as drowsiness. More recent antidepressants, such as the selective serotonin reuptake inhibitors (SSRIs) **a**, generally affect the production level of only one monoamine: for instance, Prozac prevents serotonin being reabsorbed or broken down.

ⓔ This answer is accurate, well detailed and cohesive. It is possibly slightly over-long for the 4 marks on offer, but **a** its main fault, and it is a major one, is that drug treatment is a biological therapy, while the question quite clearly calls for a psychological one. Mistakes like this could have a huge effect on the final mark and grade achieved.

**(b) Outline and evaluate biological therapies as treatments of depression.**          (20 marks)

ⓔ This question requires both descriptive and evaluative material, this time relating to biological therapies. Material on at least two biological therapies must be given; if more than two are covered, less detail would be expected.

**(b)** ECT **a** is often used to treat depression. It was actually originally designed to treat schizophrenia, but became more of an accepted treatment for depression **c**. It produces a seizure that can last up to a minute and can either be done unilaterally, where shocks are given to just one side of the head, or bilaterally, where shocks are given to both sides of the head **c**. Bilateral treatments tend to be associated with more side effects than unilateral treatments. Nowadays ECT tends to consist of mild shocks given for very brief periods and is given to a patient about two or three times a week for between 5 and 15 treatment sessions **c**. It has to be given with an anaesthetic and a muscle relaxant to prevent bone fractures. It is generally given when other treatments have failed and, there may be a risk of suicide **c**.
Another biological treatment is psychosurgery **b**, which involves irreversible destruction of localised areas of brain tissue **c**. It is not used very often **c**, generally being a last resort when other treatments have failed, and there is a high risk of self-harm.

Antunes (2009) **d** found that ECT is better than antidepressants, because quality of life was good after treatment and the patients liked the treatment. Another psychologist called Taylor (2007) **d** found that ECT made 55% of patients better and up to 90% when used with severe depressives. Side effects **e** seem worse with children, teenagers, old people and women who are pregnant, so perhaps that means ECT should not really be used with these types of people and maybe women should have a pregnancy test **e** before they have ECT, because you never know.

After 1975 ECT e went down in America when the drugs came in, but it has gone up again now, perhaps because the drugs are not really as good as people hoped they were going to be and maybe because ECT is better now than it was before. You should not use ECT e before people have been thoroughly inspected and they have given their consent to be shocked, though can a person who is really depressed ever be in a mental state where they are really able to give informed consent f?

Psychotherapy is also given to depressives sometimes and De Clerq (1999) found it was good when done by skilled nurses who had been well trained g.

🄔 The second part of the question requires at least two biological therapies to be addressed and two are, a ECT and b psychosurgery, though psychosurgery is covered only very briefly and without any evaluation. There are only 4 marks available for description here, so c far too much material is produced. This gains no extra credit and takes away from valuable time that could have been spent producing an evaluation of such biological therapies. Additionally, the student would do well to practise developing a more concise style. There are d some evaluative points made about ECT and these are generally accurate and relevant, e though not well focused or related to specific research studies. A f decent point about ethics is made, before, in the final paragraph, the student g introduces brief evaluative material on psychotherapy. Perhaps this was an attempt at comparison with biological therapies, which would have been appropriate, but the material has not been used in this fashion and therefore attracts no credit.

**(a) (AOI = 0/4) + (b) (AOI = 4/4) + (AO2/AO3 = 7/16) = 11/24 marks**

## Question 7 **Anxiety disorders (I)**

**Discuss psychological explanations of phobic disorders.**                    (24 marks)

🄔 This is a straightforward essay question taken directly from the specification. Material on at least two psychological explanations must be given; if more than two explanations are offered, less detail would be expected. There are 8 marks available for describing psychological explanations, leaving 16 marks for the evaluation, with a wealth of research evidence available to use. Material on biological explanations would not gain credit if used descriptively, but could form part of an evaluation as a comparison to psychological explanations.

### Student answer

Classical conditioning is a behaviourist explanation a that views phobias as occurring through the association of traumatic events with neutral stimuli and the resulting phobias then becoming resistant to extinction, because of the avoidance responses made to avoid feared objects or situations. Operant conditioning explains how phobias are maintained, as when avoidance responses are made, the fear element is reduced, reinforcing the avoidance responses and so making them more likely to recur a. For instance, if an individual has a phobia of water, due to a traumatic event occurring while swimming, then the phobic is likely to avoid open water, reducing the fear element and increasing the chances the sufferer will make the same avoidance response again c. Social learning theory can explain phobias as occurring through observation and imitation of others, because simply watching somebody experience a traumatic event can cause the observer to subsequently experience the fear response in the presence of the same stimulus a.

Another psychological explanation is that of the cognitive viewpoint b, where phobias are seen as originating from maladaptive thinking, for example when being in a car accident generates a belief that all cars are dangerous. Therefore the maladaptive thinking is a reaction to an anxiety-generating situation, which then becomes a phobia. An additional cognitive factor involves the tendency of those with anxiety disorders to be affected by attentional bias b. For instance, phobics concentrate their attention more on anxiety-generating stimuli than other people.

There are several forms of psychological therapies c that are used to treat phobias. Behaviourist therapies are based upon the idea that depression is a learned behaviour that can be treated by using learning theory principles, such as operant conditioning and social learning. Reinforcements are used to elevate mood and encourage participation in positive behaviours. Social reinforcement, from family members and social networks, is utilised to provide support for the depressed individual.

Psychodynamic therapies c have their origins in Freud's psychoanalytic theory and exist in varying types. Psychoanalysis c is an intensive form, consisting of several sessions a week for lengthy periods, traditionally conducted with the phobic lying on a couch. Psychoanalytic psychotherapy c is a less intensive form, consisting of fewer sessions per week and over a shorter period, with therapist and phobic in a face-to-face scenario. Psychodynamic therapies c try to reveal the repressed conflicts that are expressed as phobias so that the sufferer can have insight into the origins of their disorder and eventually arrive at a more rational understanding of events that occurred in their childhood.

Gray (1975) provided support for the behaviourist explanation d, by using the two-process theory to explain how operant conditioning can strengthen phobias acquired through classical conditioning. A phobia is first learned by a specific event being paired with the fear response and then an avoidance response is learned that reduces the fear element, thus strengthening the avoidance response. Further support for the explanation came from Ost and Hugdahl (1981) d, who reported on the case of a boy who witnessed his grandfather vomit while dying and subsequently developed a strong and persistent vomiting phobia, even contemplating suicide when feeling nauseous, supporting the idea that phobias can be acquired vicariously through social learning experiences.

A problem with the cognitive explanation e is that it is not clear whether distorted and negative thinking is a cause or an effect of a phobia. Another problem is that the explanation e is deterministic in perceiving phobias as due to psychological factors that the phobic has no control over.

ⓔ This answer is a hit-and-miss affair, containing both good and poor elements. The student addresses the need to provide descriptive material on at least two psychological explanations, detailing the a behaviourist and b cognitive viewpoints in a coherent, accurate and detailed fashion.

The student then wastes valuable examination time, gaining no extra credit, by **c** providing a description of psychological therapies for phobias, which in no way provides any additional insight into psychological explanations.

The latter part of the answer contains some good evaluative points about both **d** the behaviourist and **e** cognitive models, but evidently the student did not have enough time left to build this up into anything approaching an effective assessment of the explanations. This could easily have been achieved by further usage of research evidence and possibly even by comparison with biological explanations and inclusion of relevant ethical and methodological considerations.

**(AO1 = 8/8) + (AO2/AO3 = 6/16) = 14/24 marks**

# Question 8 Anxiety disorders (II)

**(a) Outline the clinical characteristics of one anxiety disorder.** (8 marks)

**(b) To what extent are diagnoses of anxiety disorders reliable and valid?** (16 marks)

ⓔ This type of parted question places the descriptive part of the question in one section and the evaluative in the other. Therefore in part (a) only descriptive material should be offered relating to clinical characteristics of one anxiety disorder — no marks are earned for including evaluative material. Part (b) requires an evaluation of how reliable and valid diagnoses of anxiety disorders are, and any purely descriptive material placed in this section gains no credit.

**Student answer**

**(a)** Phobias are characterised by extreme, irrational and enduring fears that cannot be controlled and involve anxiety levels far beyond any actual risk **a**. Phobic disorders are about twice as common among females, and about 10% of the population suffer from a specific phobia at some point, with most phobias originating in childhood and diminishing in strength during adulthood **a**.

Agoraphobia, a fear of open spaces, is very common, often occurring with panic disorder, where the sufferer endures the panic disorder first and then the anxiety generated makes them feel vulnerable about being in open spaces. Social phobias **b** are also common, generally involving being over-anxious about social situations, such as talking in public. There are also simple phobias **b** where sufferers have fears of specific things and environments, for example astraphobia, an extreme fear of thunderstorms. Animal phobias tend to have the earliest onset, followed by other simple phobias, social phobias and then agoraphobia **b**.

Symptoms include persistent, excessive fear of the phobic object, recognising that the fear is exaggerated and avoiding the phobic situation or object by making avoidance responses. These avoidance responses are generally so extreme that intense disruption occurs to everyday work and social functioning **c**.

ⓔ This answer is excellent: just about the right length for the marks and time available, containing sufficient detail in an accurate and coherent style and also containing plenty of breadth about the **a** general characteristics, **b** subtypes and **c** symptoms of phobic disorders.

**(b)** Silverman (2001) **a** generated support for the test–retest reliability of phobic disorders **e**, when finding that, after administering the Anxiety Disorders Interview Schedule, results indicated similar diagnoses for both specific and social phobias. Further support **b** came from Mataix-Cols (2005) **a**, who found internal consistency to be high when using the Work and Social Adjustment Scale on 205 phobic patients **e**, although simple phobics had less consistent ratings across WSAS items, suggesting some items were less relevant to their disorder.

Support for the reliability of OCD diagnoses **f** came from Geller (2006) **a**, who found the Child Behaviour Checklist to be reliable and to have acceptable psychometric properties that help discriminate children with OCD. This support was strengthened **b** by Di Nardo and Barlow (1987) **a**, who found that the principal diagnosis of OCD **f** was associated with excellent diagnostic reliability, scoring an 80% concordance rate, second only to that of simple phobias among anxiety and mood disorders. The diagnosis of OCD **f** would also appear to have good inter-rater reliability **b**, as Foa (1987) **a**, using Likert scales, obtained strong correlations among patients', therapists' and independent observers' ratings of various OCD features, including fear, avoidance and compulsion severity.

One limitation of the assessment of inter-rater reliability **c** is that it generally involves one rater interviewing a patient and another observing the same interview either live or on video. Therefore both diagnoses are based on the identical information given in the interview, which not surprisingly yields high levels of reliability. Perhaps a better method **d** would be for one rater to perform an interview and the second rater to perform a separate independent interview on the same patient.

An additional consideration **c** is that research studies tend to differ in the assessment of reliability, even when the same measuring scales are used. Early assessments of the Anxiety Disorder Interview Schedule found low levels of reliability for phobic disorders, while later studies found high levels, suggesting it was the revision of measuring scales that led to improved reliability of diagnosis.

🄴 This answer contains an excellent evaluation of the reliability of diagnoses of anxiety disorders, **a** first through research evidence where the content is well selected, expressed in a very coherent fashion, includes accurate detail and **b** is generally built up into a sophisticated and elaborated assessment and, second, **c** through limitations of how reliability is actually determined, with **d** a method of resolving one of these limitations suggested. Material on both **e** phobias and **f** OCD is included and this is fine, as the question is not worded in such a way as to limit students to writing about only one anxiety disorder, though that approach would have been perfectly acceptable. The big drawback to the answer is that there is no consideration of the validity of diagnoses, which the question specifically calls for. This limits access to the full range of marks available, as it is considered to be partial performance.

**(a) (AO1 =8/8) + (b) (AO2/AO3 = 10/16) = 18/24 marks**

# Question 9 Anxiety disorders (III)

**(a) Outline one psychological therapy for the treatment of OCD.** (4 marks)

ⓔ This requires only descriptive material relating to one psychological therapy for the treatment of one anxiety disorder, so any evaluative material produced here will not gain credit. If more than one psychological therapy were to be offered, all would be marked, but only the best one would be credited.

### Student answer

**(a)** The most common psychological treatment for OCD these days is cognitive behavioural therapy (CBT) **a**. Treatment occurs about once every 1 to 2 weeks **b**, for between 5 and 20 sessions in total **b**. The main aim of CBT is to help patients identify irrational and maladaptive thinking patterns and change them to rational, adaptive ones **b**. Thinking is seen as underpinning feelings and behaviour **b**, so if modes of thinking are changed, feelings and behaviour should also change for the better. Sometimes the drawing of diagrams that demonstrate links between thinking, emotions and behaviour is used to facilitate this process **b**. A special kind of CBT for OCD is habituation training **a**, which is aimed at changing obsessional thinking by getting sufferers to relive obsessional thoughts repeatedly in order to reduce the anxiety created **b**.

ⓔ This answer is excellent, **a** providing relevant material that is coherently expressed, with **b** a good deal of accurate detail. This is easily enough to earn the marks on offer.

**(b) Outline and evaluate biological therapies as treatments of OCD.** (20 marks)

ⓔ This question requires both descriptive and evaluative material, this time relating to biological therapies. Material on at least two biological therapies must be given; if more than two are covered, less detail would be expected.

**(b)** One biological treatment for OCD is drug medication. Anxiolytics **a**, such as the benzodiazepine Valium, work by increasing the effect of the neurotransmitter GABA and thus reducing anxiety levels. Antidepressants **b**, such as the SSRIs, elevate levels of the neurotransmitter serotonin and again have an anxiety-reducing effect. Another type of drug that has proved effective against OCD is the antipsychotics **c**; these have the effect of lowering dopamine levels. Beta-blockers **d** have also had some success in reducing the physical symptoms of anxiety disorders. They work by countering the rise in blood pressure and heart rate often associated with anxiety, by lowering adrenaline and noradrenaline production.

Support for drug treatment for OCD came from Beroqvist (1999) **e**, who investigated the effect of low doses of the antipsychotic drug risperidone in treating OCD, finding treatment to be effective due to the drug's dopamine-lowering effect. Further support **h** came from Piccinelli (1995) **e**, who performed a meta-analysis of 36 studies assessing the worth of antidepressants as a treatment for OCD. Piccinelli found them to be effective in the short-term treatment of the disorder, with 61% showing improved symptoms with the tricyclic antidepressant clomipramine and 28% with the newer SSRI medications, both treatments proving more beneficial than non-serotonergic drugs. Additional support came from Flament (1985) h, who tested the ability of the antidepressant drug clomipramine to address the symptoms of childhood OCD in 19 patients, finding the drug to be superior over a 5-week period to placebo treatment, so strengthening the argument for drug treatments e.

However g, drug treatments cannot really be regarded as a cure for OCD, as once drug-taking stops, symptoms tend to reappear. On the other hand f h, drug treatments are widely used to treat the symptoms of OCD, as they are a cost-effective and user-friendly form of treatment, with people used to swallowing pills for illnesses. However g h, it can be argued that drug treatments should not be used to treat OCD, because of the risk of side effects and the tendency of antidepressants to produce heightened levels of suicidal thinking, considered alongside the effectiveness of psychological treatments. A big issue i with the use of drug medication for OCD is that many within the psychiatric community see the widespread use of drug treatments as being fuelled by the powerful influence of the drug-producing companies who stand to make huge profits from their application. This opinion is backed up somewhat h by the fact that the latest generation of antidepressants have consistently proven to be not as effective as older varieties.

ⓔ This is also excellent. A brief outline of various drug therapies, namely a anxiolytics, b antidepressants, c antipsychotics and d beta-blockers is provided (which meets the question's requirement to offer more than one therapy) and these are accurate and detailed enough to easily earn the 4 marks on offer for the descriptive content. The evaluation uses e research evidence and points based on f strengths and g weaknesses to build an effective h commentary, such as that concerning the i power of drug companies to promote drug therapies.

**(a) (AOI = 4/4) + (b) (AOI = 4/4) + (AO2/AO3 = 16/16) = 24/24 marks**

## Knowledge check answers

1  Type I schizophrenia is an acute type, where symptoms appear suddenly following stressful incidents, and is characterised by positive symptoms, where an excess or distortion of normal functioning usually occurs, such as thought disorders. Type II schizophrenia is a chronic type, where symptoms appear over a prolonged period with sufferers becoming increasingly disturbed, and is characterised by negative symptoms, where there is a lessening or loss of normal functioning, such as apathy. Type I schizophrenia has a better prospect for recovery.

2  There's no such thing as a 'normal' schizophrenic exhibiting 'usual' symptoms, as several subtypes exist, each with differing symptoms. As symptoms overlap, different classification systems disagree as to how many subtypes there may be, making categorisation of schizophrenia problematic.

3  Research suggests that reliability of diagnosis was low, especially when practitioners used different classification systems, but has improved due to the introduction of more up-to-date classification systems. Some research indicates that reliable diagnosis of schizophrenia is so difficult to attain that it suggests schizophrenia as a separate, identifiable disorder does not exist.

4  Some research studies indicate that schizophrenia may not be a definable, separate disorder, making diagnosis of it invalid, which is supported by studies suggesting that several types of schizophrenia exist. However, other research implies that diagnosis is valid if performed upon key symptom dimensions. There is also a possibility that invalid diagnoses are made due to cultural bias when diagnosing schizophrenia.

5  (a) One genetic explanation sees schizophrenia as caused by hereditary means, while an alternative genetic explanation is that several genes are involved in determining vulnerability levels to the disorder, with environmental triggers needed to precipitate the disorder. (b) The evolutionary explanation perceives schizophrenia as having an adaptive value, with the disorder providing dynamic leaders essential to the survival and prosperity of new groups, following group splitting in response to environmental demands. (c) The biochemical explanation sees high levels of dopamine in the mesolimbic dopamine system linked to positive symptoms, and high levels in the mesocortical dopamine system linked to negative symptoms. Abnormal levels of the neurotransmitter glutamate in combination with dopamine may also trigger onset of schizophrenia.

6  (a) Neuroanatomical explanations see enlarged ventricles as a cause of schizophrenia, especially with Type II schizophrenia. (b) Pregnancy factors suggest that viral infections contracted by pregnant women increase vulnerability to the disorder in their fetuses, as does damage during pregnancy, and birth complications.

7  (a) Behaviourist explanations see schizophrenia as a learned condition via operant conditioning, with sufferers being reinforced for their bizarre behaviours and thus repeating them. Additionally, the attention schizophrenic behaviour brings is also reinforcing. Escaping from reality into schizophrenia may also be reinforcing by escaping real-world pressures. Social learning may also occur where schizophrenic family members are observed and imitated. (b) Psychodynamic explanations see schizophrenia as regression to a childlike state of primary narcissism, due to an increase in sexual or aggressive urges in early adulthood. Schizophrenics are perceived as having experienced interpersonal regression or interpersonal withdrawal, with stress, especially from family tensions, as a contributory factor.

8  (a) Cognitive explanations see faulty thought processes as the basis of schizophrenia, either directly or indirectly via physical brain abnormalities. Schizophrenics may not be able to filter out irrelevant sensory information, or may suffer confusion between information stored in memory and new incoming information, leading to delusions and hallucinations. (b) Sociocultural explanations see family and social environments as the basis for schizophrenia. The degree of expressed emotion within a family, such as hostility and excess concern, may contribute to the maintenance of schizophrenia, while individuals in lower classes may experience more social stressors and thus be increasingly vulnerable to the condition.

9  Research suggests that ECT is effective, though not as effective as drug treatments and indeed works best in conjunction with drug treatments. ECT is especially effective against cases of schizophrenia that do not respond to drug treatments, though it is not a long-term solution to treating the disorder, with relapses a common occurrence.

10  Research suggests that both first- and second-generation antipsychotics are effective in treating schizophrenia, with some studies, though not all, suggesting that second-generation antipsychotics produce greater symptom relief and lower relapse rates. However, both forms produce side effects to such an extent that discontinuation of treatment often occurs. Drugs are familiar to patients, trusted and relatively cost-effective.

11  Research suggests that (a) the behavioural therapy of token economy reduces negative symptoms, though mainly with patients showing initiative and cooperation with hospital staff. Token economies also reduce weight loss associated with taking antipsychotics. Improvements may not continue when tokens are withdrawn. Research suggests that (b) psychodynamic therapies have little, if any, positive effect, though they can be useful in conjunction with drug therapies, but only for patients able to express themselves verbally. Problem-based home-treatment psychotherapy seems superior to hospital-applied versions in reducing symptoms and improving social functioning and is relatively cost-effective.

12  Research suggests that CBT is highly effective in treating schizophrenia, reducing both positive and negative symptoms (though more so with positive symptoms) and in speeding up recovery rates of acutely ill patients, as well as being associated with lower relapse rates than with other treatments. CBT does not reduce the intensity of hallucinations but makes them seem less of a threat. Treatment is effective only if there is empathy between clinicians and patients.

**13** Using the DSM-IV classification system, for depression to be diagnosed, five of the eight listed symptoms must be apparent every day for at least 2 weeks, of which at least one symptom must be a constant depressed mood or lessened interest in daily activities. An impairment in general functioning must also be evident that is not explicable by another medical condition or environmental event.

**14** Endogenous depression is associated with abnormal biochemical and hormonal factors within sufferers, while reactive depression is a reaction to external environmental factors, such as elevated levels of stress.

**15** Unipolar depression manifests itself purely as depression while, with bipolar depression, sufferers alternate between periods of depression and mania, which is characterised by high arousal and, occasionally, delusions and hallucinations. Mania can occur in some sufferers without incidents of depression.

**16** Research suggests that the inter-rater reliability of depression where clinicians independently agree with each other's diagnosis, is high. Test–retest reliability is also high, suggesting that diagnosis is reliable over time. These findings suggest the inventories used to diagnose depression are reliable diagnostic tools.

**17** Although early research indicated problems with the validity of diagnosis, more recent research, using more up-to-date classification systems and diagnostic scales, suggests that validity is now highly valid, though some commonly-used scales have low validity. Some research indicates that, while particular scales are valid diagnostic tools, they cannot assess the severity of depression.

**18** (a) One genetic explanation perceives depression as being caused by hereditary means, while an alternative genetic explanation is that several genes are involved in determining vulnerability levels to the disorder, with environmental triggers needed to precipitate the disorder. (b) Evolutionary explanations perceive an adaptive value to depression linked to survival, with the rank theory seeing depression as a reaction to defeat in dominance battles that serves to protect an individual from further harm, while the social navigation theory sees depression as helping individuals to realise that changes are required in social networks. Depression also motivates social partners to provide support to promote inclusive fitness within a social group.

**19** The biochemical explanation sees abnormally low levels of the monoamine neurotransmitters serotonin, noradrenaline and dopamine as causative factors of depression. Hormonal changes may also play a role, with high levels of the stress hormone cortisol being linked to the disorder. It may be that abnormal brain structures affect biochemistry, which then leads to depression.

**20** (a) The behaviourist explanation sees depression as learned from environmental experiences. Negative events such as relationship dissolution can lead to less positive reinforcements through enjoyable experiences, resulting in depression. Depression is also explained by operant conditioning through the reinforcing attention it brings, as well as by social learning theory (SLT), through the observation and imitation of depressive models that are reinforced. (b) The psychodynamic explanation sees depression as originating in melancholic childhood experiences of loss and rejection, with similar adult experiences leading to a reliving of such childhood loss.

**21** (a) Cognitive explanations see depression as caused by dysfunctional beliefs and cognitive vulnerabilities, such as the negative triad, where individuals possess self-defeating negative thought patterns about themselves that lead to depression. Depression can also result from attributing failures and shortcomings to oneself rather than external factors, with such people also prone to feelings of hopelessness. (b) Sociocultural explanations focus on family and social environments, with special emphasis on life event stressors that can trigger and maintain depression. Those with reduced social networks and interpersonal skills are also seen as more vulnerable to depression.

**22** Research suggests that antidepressants are effective, as they work better than placebos, and recent research suggests that cytokine-based antidepressants may increase drug treatment effectiveness. Psychological treatments are more effective, but drugs are preferred, as they are familiar, trusted and cost-effective. Antidepressants are associated with suicide attempts among children and adolescents and the new generation of SSRIs, such as Prozac, may work no better than placebos, with critics accusing drug companies of suppressing evidence that casts doubts on their effectiveness, to protect profits.

**23** Research suggests that ECT is effective, as it is a superior treatment to placebos and antidepressants, even for severe and resistant forms, and that it improves quality of life and is perceived positively by patients. Unilateral treatments cause less memory loss but bilateral treatments produce higher symptom relief. ECT can produce side effects such as memory loss and has a high relapse rate, which suggests it is not long-term effective. Side effects are more severe in the young, the elderly and pregnant women. ECT is especially perceived as an appropriate treatment for patients non-responsive to other forms of treatments and those at high risk of suicide.

**24** (a) Research suggests that BAT is tolerable, cost-effective and equal in performance to CBT, with a low drop-out rate and superior long-term outcomes than with antidepressants. BAT is also modifiable to the needs of different patients. Structured learning therapy, based on stress inoculation therapy (SIT), is preferable to traditional psychotherapies, improving psychosocial functioning across age ranges and ethnic groupings. (b) Psychodynamic therapies are effective when delivered by experienced, supervised staff and work well in conjunction with drug therapies. Psychotherapy seems especially helpful in elderly patients with low cognitive functioning and modern forms of the therapy have proven as effective as CBT.

**25** Research suggests CBT is the most effective form of treatment for depression and produces few side effects, though is not suitable for all patients, such as those who have trouble concentrating or discussing their inner feelings, where depressive symptoms can be strengthened. CBT is relatively expensive, but self-help versions of the treatment are cheaper and thus more cost-effective.

**26** When anxiety levels become extreme, enduring, irrational and uncontrollable, then they will be so maladaptive as to interfere with normal day-to-day functioning and thus be classed as phobias.

**27** OCD is classed as an anxiety disorder, as the obsessions involved with OCD consist of forbidden or unsuitable ideas and visual images that involve high degrees of anxiety, while compulsions involve intense, uncontrollable urges to perform repetitively tasks and behaviours that sufferers realise are inappropriate but which cannot be consciously controlled, thus resulting in high-level anxiety.

**28** Research suggests that the test–retest reliability of phobias in children is good, implying diagnosis is reliable over time. A commonly used scale, the Work and Social Adjustment Scale, was found to have high internal reliability between clinicians for work and social adjustment, though less so for simple phobias. With OCD, research suggests high inter-rater reliability of diagnosis between clinicians and for the diagnostic scales used. Reliability for both phobias and OCD has improved with revision of diagnostic procedures and measuring tools.

**29** Research indicates that validity of diagnosis of phobias is low, as sufferers often have other anxiety disorders too and separate subtypes of phobias, such as social phobias, often do not appear to be separate subtypes at all. As treatment outcomes are often similar, this also suggests low predictive validity. For OCD, research also suggests validity problems, with OCD often overlapping with Tourette's syndrome, suggesting OCD not to be a separate disorder, while commonly-used scales, like the Yale-Brown Obsessive Compulsive scale, have problems in accurately measuring the components of OCD.

**30** (a) One genetic explanation perceives both phobias and OCD as being caused by hereditary means, while an alternative genetic explanation is that several genes are involved in determining vulnerability levels to the disorders, with environmental triggers needed to precipitate them. (b) Evolutionary explanations see an adaptive advantage to anxiety disorders linked to survival, or they would have died out. Phobias are seen as stimulating the body to avoid danger, while OCD rituals help prevent infection and increase alertness and vigilance.

**31** Biochemical factors are seen as playing a part in determining individual levels of vulnerability to anxiety disorders, with environmental triggers also having a contributory role. Abnormal levels of the amino acid GABA, involved in the control of anxiety levels, are associated with phobias, as are low levels of the neurotransmitter serotonin, which are additionally linked to OCD, along with elevated levels of dopamine.

**32** (a) Behaviourist explanations see anxiety disorders as learned from environmental experiences. Classical conditioning sees phobias as acquired through traumatic events becoming associated with neutral stimuli, while operant conditioning explains how avoidance responses are reinforcing, thus helping to maintain phobias. SLT explains phobias as acquired via observation and imitation. With OCD, compulsions can be responses learned via operant conditioning, which reduce anxiety brought on through obsessions, thus maintaining the disorder, while the superstition hypothesis explains how bodily actions are repeated due to being associated with a reinforcer. (b) Psychodynamic explanations view phobias as offering protection against repressed anxieties, which displace on to phobic objects that symbolise the original anxiety. OCD meanwhile is seen as an exaggeration of the anal personality type, with obsessions also seen as defence mechanisms against anxiety-causing thoughts. OCD is also explained by ego defence mechanisms protecting against the anxiety produced by unacceptable urges of the id.

**33** (a) Cognitive explanations see phobias as originating from maladaptive thinking that occurs as a reaction to anxiety-generating situations. OCD is explained as sufferers having impaired, persistent thought processes that lead to self-blame and heightened anxiety, with behaviours that decrease the anxiety from obsessive thoughts becoming compulsions that are difficult to control. (b) Sociocultural explanations see cultural factors as influencing phobias, as many are culture-specific. Although cultural factors are not seen as a key factor in OCD, they do influence actual symptoms, as these vary cross-culturally. Social factors can also help develop anxiety disorders through family dynamics.

**34** Research suggests that SSRIs are effective against the physical symptoms of phobias and that BZs also suppress symptoms in agoraphobics and social phobics, though they can be addictive and incur increased anxiety on withdrawal. MAOIs reduce social anxiety, though they can increase hypertension. With OCD, antidepressants have proved an effective short-term treatment, while the antipsychotic drug risperidone works by lowering dopamine activity. However, although cost-effective, side effects can occur and symptoms tend to reappear when treatment stops.

**35** Although generally a 'last resort' treatment due to its irreversible nature, research suggests that psychosurgery is a long-term effective treatment against agoraphobia, with only mild personality changes evident. Psychosurgery is also effective against social phobias, though severe side effects can occur. With OCD, limbic leucotomies have proved long-term effective, though gamma capsulotomies benefit only a few. Psychosurgery can reduce OCD symptoms but is associated with severe side effects, such as seizures.

**36** (a) SD and implosion have proved effective against phobias, as has virtual reality exposure therapy, which, because it occurs completely within a clinical setting, has additional benefits of less exposure to harm and embarrassment and more control gained over phobic stimuli. All these strategies require an ability to use relaxation strategies, and SD additionally requires a vivid imagination. OCD patients benefit from in vivo SD and from ERP, which also incurs low relapse rates. Self-directed forms of ERP are effective for mild forms of OCD, as well as being relatively cost-effective, though ERP treatments are associated with high drop-out rates. (b) With psychodynamic therapies, PGT is effective against social phobias and treating specific phobias with psychodynamic therapy is as effective as in vivo behaviourist treatments. Psychodynamic therapies can be combined with other therapies and suit all age ranges, though psychotherapy benefits only those with insight into their condition and the ability to express themselves. Research suggests that psychotherapy is generally ineffective in treating OCD.

**37** Child-focused CBT and CBT with parental involvement are both long-term effective in treating social phobias in children and CBT is generally effective against many phobias, though some phobias seem resistant to the treatment. With OCD, CBT seems more effective than drug therapies but works better when combined with drug therapies. HT seems ineffective as, although it works well within treatment sessions, it does not work well between sessions. For anxiety disorders in general, CBT produces few side effects, can be used continually to stop symptoms recurring, but requires empathetic, well-trained staff and does not suit those who cannot or will not discuss their inner feelings.